BREAKING FREE

BREAKING FREE

How to Quit Your Job and Start Your Own Business

Chris Lauer

Westport, Connecticut
London

Library of Congress Cataloging-in-Publication Data

Lauer, Chris, 1966–
   Breaking free : how to quit your job and start your own business / Chris Lauer.
     p. cm.
   Includes bibliographical references and index.
   ISBN: 978-0-313-35534-9 (alk. paper)
   1. New business enterprises—United States.   2. Small business—United
States—Management.   3. Entrepreneurship—United States.   I. Title.
   HD62.5.L377   2009
   658.1′1—dc22   2008041029

British Library Cataloguing in Publication Data is available.

Library of Congress Catalog Card Number: 2008041029
ISBN: 978-0-313-35534-9

First published in 2009

Praeger Publishers, 88 Post Road West, Westport, CT 06881
An imprint of Greenwood Publishing Group, Inc.
www.praeger.com

Printed in the United States of America

The paper used in this book complies with the
Permanent Paper Standard issued by the National
Information Standards Organization (Z39.48–1984).

10 9 8 7 6 5 4 3 2 1

To Michelle

Contents

Introduction

The Clock Is Ticking

determine vt. *1 to define limitations or make defined 2 to investigate and then make a choice; to decide*

determined adj. *1 having set one's mind on a specific course; resolved 2 steadfast; unfaltering*

When my pregnant wife, Michelle, and I were looking for a house to buy in Eureka, California, in 1999, two of the charms that helped us choose our future home were its lovely neighborhood and the friendly people who lived there. On our first visit, we met Jack, who lived directly across the street in a little pink house with an immaculate yard. Jack soon became one of our favorite people. He showed our two young daughters all of the varieties of flowers in his well-tended garden, and we quickly discovered that he was an awesome neighbor. A few months after we moved in, Jack—a healthy man in his early 60s—reached the day when he could finally retire from his engineering job at a local firm. Less than a week off the job, this physically fit bicycle rider, kind neighbor, and avid gardener suddenly and sadly had a massive heart attack and died.

Although we had only been friends for a couple of months, Jack's death had a profound effect on me. I instantly realized how suddenly death puts an end to the best intentions. Life was shorter than I had previously thought, and getting shorter every day. The speed of my once unlimited commodity, time, suddenly moved much faster than before, making each day more precious than the last. Jack's death made me plainly aware of the priceless fragility of life and the tiny amount of time I had left to make the most of it. I decided to improve the time I had left. I vowed to improve my time at home, which was often playing second fiddle to my work life. I also promised myself that I would strive to improve my daily working life by aligning it better with my dreams of independence.

Most of us work hard all our lives to create a comfortable living—and perhaps eventual retirement—sacrificing our time to work for others or ourselves so we can efficiently produce something of value to somebody. This earns us our pay so we can buy the things we need to survive and thrive. Working can either give our lives meaning or simply provide us with the cash to buy the things that give it meaning on our time off. Many people have found that starting and running a business gives their lives greater meaning and satisfaction than they would have had if they had continued to work for other people.

Work is an inevitability that is here to stay for most of us, so it is wise to spend our time working in ways that make us happiest. It is also smart to mull over the idea of self-employment now and then, just to see where we stand, and how we might benefit. In this free society, created as a result of much hard work and entrepreneurial thinking, we all have a choice to make: We can either collect a paycheck from somebody else in return for doing the work they require, or we can create our own paycheck in return for doing the work that we require. We can also create a combination of both, but essentially we can choose either to work for others or work for ourselves.

The people whose stories and ideas are collected in this book, including myself, are people who started our own successful businesses. We quit doing what we were doing to make a positive change: We became self-employed. We love to work for ourselves. Reaching self-employment was an exciting journey for each of us. With years of experience, each of these friends and family members discovered the joy of self-employment. All of the stories are different but similar, and each person has his or her own unique motivations to make his or her business work. Jack's memory helps me remember why the hard work of running a business is worth it, even during the greatest struggles: Time is short.

Jack's sudden death instilled in me a dedication to making positive choices about how I spend my working time and what I am doing while I earn my keep. As I contemplate the unexpected death of my neighbor, I realize that I need to spend my time at work engaged in pursuits that make me happy and satisfied rather than those that only pay my bills, because every one of these moments may be the last one I get.

Don't Wait Until It Is Too Late

If financial responsibilities require you to work to earn a living, too, I assume that we have more things in common than we have differences. I also imagine that most of my thoughts about life, mortality, and making the most of working life are universal. Although our personal attributes and business conditions might differ in a million ways, I believe anyone can benefit from the different lessons that have helped me and the other self-employed people in this book exercise our choices about whom we serve. The people I profile here have chosen to work for themselves, serving their customers and clients instead of working for others and serving bosses as employees. If you are thinking about taking this journey, I'm hoping that after you've read the stories compiled here, you are better prepared to ask yourself, "If they can do it, why can't I?" Then I hope you are better prepared to look deeply into your own motivations, dreams, and aspirations to develop a vision for earning a more satisfying living as your own boss than you are currently earning while working for others.

Of course, individual circumstances will determine the usefulness of the tips and techniques included in this book, so please don't make a rash decision to quit your job before you have lined up everything necessary to do it smoothly and effectively. Make sure it will be an improvement to your life. And don't sacrifice anything you will regret later. Otherwise, jumping the gun will simply leave you with fewer choices about your future and the destiny of your precious moments. Underlying all of these diverse and sometimes opposing ideas is a brazen attempt to increase choices, which naturally increases happiness for independent-minded people like me, or us.

For some people, more choices mean more headaches. The responsibility of making important decisions can be daunting. If you seek fewer choices and decisions to fill your time because decision making stresses you out, then be warned: Self-employment will not enhance your happiness or satisfaction. It increases the choices and decisions that accompany all forms of independence. You can revisit the idea of self-employment when you get a better grip on your capacity to make choices.

Many wonderful people enjoy the comfort of a job working for others, filled with parameters and processes set by other people. These are the satisfied and powerful people who serve their managers and executives well, either trotting boldly up the corporate ladder or riding it out until retirement. But if you are like me, and you feel agitated by the confines of parameters and processes chosen by others, and feel that you are not living up to your personal potential because you sense that bad decisions from above are keeping you from demonstrating your true value and mission in life, self-employment might be a dream that tugs at you daily. If the entrepreneurial bug is a persistent pest in the back of your brain, don't smash it; save it. Nurture it and feed it. Help it grow with research and resources. Make it a pet project that leads to more diverse experiments with making money on the side. Investigate the elements of your own personality or interests that can be developed and grown to support themselves through hard work in an industry you love.

Incubate Your Plans

After incubating a new business idea for a few months or years, a moment comes when its possibilities for profit become apparent. It is a wonderful moment when the stars are aligned, the groundwork has been prepared, and the culmination of much thought and preparation comes to a head. It could even be the best day of your life! It is the day you tell your boss that you are resigning from your current position: Thanks for everything, but no thanks. I quit.

The day you quit your job can be the most exhilarating day of your life—one that you will cherish like no other. It could also be the scariest day of your life. But with the forethought and planning described in these pages by people who have done it themselves, you can ease much of that fear. Hopefully, on the day that you officially become your own boss, all your worries will be kept at bay by the satisfaction and joy of this momentous occasion. This is the day that you transformed all of your experiences, skills, training, and planning into a job that will fill your life with pride and happiness, a job that might even exist long after you are dead.

Do It Yourself

The day I quit my job and started my own business was one of the most exciting days of my life. Any natural strangeness of the rare occasion was overcome by a warm feeling of familiarity. The idea of working for myself as a writer actually stems from experiences I've been having and skills I've been developing since I was a teenager. For example, the self-employment opportunity I cultivated uses most of the same talents I've been honing for decades.

As a big fan of the do-it-yourself (DIY) movement that was taking root in the mid-1980s, I published my first magazine when I was 20. The consensus among my high school and college friends, who contributed to its contents of cartoons, art, stories, and poetry, was to call our publication *Temper Tantrum Anthems* as an expression of the youthful angst and pride we all shared.

I made three hundred copies of the twenty-four-page first issue on the photocopy machine at the hospital where my mother worked. I borrowed a stapler and bound the pages on my bedroom floor. Although I gave most of the mini-magazines, or "zines," away for free, I also sold a few of them for one dollar each through the mail to people who had read a review of it in *Maximum Rocknroll*, a monthly magazine from San Francisco that encourages DIY music, art, and thought. Our readers liked *Temper Tantrum Anthems*, so my friends and I created five more issues over the next few years, usually printed inexpensively on a copy machine at school.

Although I published the magazine/comicbook/fanzine/chapbook as a hobby and way to commemorate the original work my friends and I were creating during a very productive period in our young lives, little did I realize that I was actually building a very solid foundation on which I would eventually base the rest of my life and career until today, more than twenty years later. What seemed at the time as a terrific way to interact with my friends as well as people I had never met before has actually become my way of life: spreading words and pictures.

Prove It

Today, I am a freelance writer and editor. I started my own editorial services business three years ago, but it's not the first time I have worked for myself and made a living doing what I love.

More than a decade ago, I was an independent publisher, writer, and editor, and my daily work today is not much different. Times and careers change, but they also stay the same in many ways. My career as a writer, reporter, artist, and creative type has had many twists and turns through a variety of jobs and experiences across the country. Through it all, I have been adding to the skills and abilities that allow me to make a great living as a freelancer and a business owner. I believe luck and fate have had less to do with my success than my continuing embrace of change and my ability to stay focused on the things that I love to do the most: creating and connecting.

The inevitability of change is one of the underlying premises of this book that many individuals who believe in the status quo might find disconcerting. It is easy to be resistant to the dynamics of life because of illusions of stability. Many people have learned to look askance at change and distrust those who purport to be harbingers of it. That's good. A little skepticism is important to any learning process. Hopefully, after reading how I have been able to combine stasis and change into a yin-yang balance throughout my career, and how others have combined tradition and change to improve their lives and careers, you will reconsider your fear or trepidation of change. Helping others build a healthier relationship with the possibilities of positive change is, perhaps, the true underlying purpose of this book. But I digress.

Today, as I sit here looking over my laptop monitor, out the window of my house at a lovely summer day, it is easy to appreciate how good I have it after so many years spent working in a corporate environment where I had no windows through which to see the day as I toiled away in my oppressive cubicle. Now, my satisfaction goes deeper than merely a nice view of trees, flowers, and sky. At the moment, my first book, *The Management Gurus*, is printing on Portfolio's presses: A profound satisfaction that is only possible because of my choice to break free from my employer—and turn that employer, on my own terms, into my favorite client.

You are currently holding in your hands my second book, reading what is basically a culmination of the knowledge, skills, and techniques that have transformed me from a college student sitting on the bedroom floor of my parent's house, stapling together the pages of my first publication, to a business owner sitting in the spare bedroom of his own home making a great living by doing essentially the same thing on a larger scale with newer technology.

My life is truly better today than it was before I quit my cubicle job. It's not just better because I have reached many of my career goals and feel like I am beginning to truly enjoy my work more than ever before, but it is improved because I have been able to nicely balance my time at work with my time involved in the lives of my family members and friends. The flexibility of working for myself has opened up vast new possibilities for creating better relationships and memories with the people in my life.

Using the lessons I have learned from classes, jobs, experiences, and the mentoring of friends and family, I have been able to provide a comfortable living for my family and myself for many years. Although my profession of choice is journalism, I believe the keys to success that I share can be applied to any profession, industry, or career. I think these lessons can work for anybody willing to do the hard work it takes to prepare to quit a job and perform the daily hard work self-employment requires.

We can all become more self-reliant. Although we have different paths and live in a variety of locations, the entrepreneurs featured in this book have all mastered self-reliance at their own levels. I believe their inspiring successes can be similarly replicated by anyone with the courage, strength, and desire to make a positive difference in his or her own life through self-employment. By taking the proper actions to become more self-sufficient, I believe anyone can improve his or her job satisfaction, create healthier relationships, and enjoy more personal happiness.

Capitalizing on properly planned self-employment opportunities also requires recognizing them when they appear and nurturing them until they come to fruition. These entrepreneurs offer clues about what those crucial opportunities looked like in their own lives. I hope this collection of stories and characters can help you focus on some of the things that helped us reach our goal of job independence.

If average folks like us can do it, you probably can, too. Even if you choose to stay in the job you are in for the next several decades, it can pay to plant a seed today that one day might grow to help you survive and thrive, whether you quit your job or your job suddenly slips out from under you.

Clear Your Head

It is not easy to pull together all the elements of the self-employment puzzle to form a successful business, but a clear head is a good place to start. Nothing can help you more than some quality time with yourself at your best. Sit down and think. Here's my prescription for a better plan for anything: Take yourself out of your daily grind, remove yourself from the millions of distractions on your desk or in your ear. Turn off your devices, sit down somewhere comfortable, and think about your life. This might seem the most obvious of the many bits of advice offered here, but its simplicity is as important as the positive possibilities it creates. How do you know who you are until you take a good look at yourself in the proverbial mirror? Who do you want to be when you grow up?

Take some time to think about yourself, who you are, who you want to be, what makes you happy, who you want to emulate, where you want to go, and how you are going to get there. Who do you want to help or influence? What role do you want to play in your community? What direction do you want to go? How do you like to spend your time? What industry appeals to you? How can you create value for customers? This book describes the answers a variety of people have discovered to these and many other questions.

After thinking deeply about yourself, you will be better prepared to set your focus on a point in the future where you want to be. This goal—a shining light that will guide you during your most chaotic days in other people's organizations—gives you the direction you need to travel to reach your full potential. That distant star on the horizon is the star you can become if you return again and again to that place where you are soberly thinking about your future. Where do you want to be in five, ten, or fifty years? Thanks to modern science, we are living longer. With all of these great new tools and gadgets, and a smart plan for the future, we can improve these extra years by building a job that will keep us happier than we were while working for others. The people I write about in this book describe how they reached out and grabbed some of this happiness for themselves.

Think It Over

Your future is not that long from now. Some clear-headed thinking can help you build a firm foundation for the valuable planning you will need to get where you want to go. Once you've got a plan and a direction to face, then you can turn all of your gizmos back on. Perhaps you will use them to network and communicate in an effort to build the relationships that can help you get your self-employment adventure moving forward.

Although serendipity and chance often play a role in the stories of many business startups, forethought and planning are still central to success. Demonstrating this through real people and their true stories, this book also contains my own story and ideas about quitting and starting a new business. I hope these strategies and experiences can help you think about and create your own answers to the questions about careers and happiness we all ask ourselves. Once you have read about my family, my friends, and me, I hope you take some time to evaluate your own life and career while imagining where a self-employment opportunity might fit in. I hope your adventure is as exciting and satisfying as the stories I share in these pages.

I believe wholeheartedly that I'm not much different than the millions of other Baby Boomers, Gen Xers, Gen Ys, and so on. With so many billions of people on the planet these days, more than likely, I'm much like you. We might differ in location, community, or upbringing, but I'll bet we share far more characteristics than we do not share. I successfully quit my job and started my own; you probably can, too.

I have organized this book on the standard who–what–when–where–how–why formula I learned in journalism school. I also examine connecting, hiring, selling, and growing once your business gets rolling. Assuming you will succeed in your journey, I also address retiring and making the most of the future.

Before I get to the reporting, I share my own self-employment adventure. Then I introduce more than one dozen of my friends and family members who have helped me learn what it takes to quit a job, start your own business, and love it. These people have done it. Although they are all important to me, the biggest part of this story is you.

Don't leave yourself out of the equation for success. Embrace what makes you unique. And enjoy what makes you just like everyone else. Believe in yourself. It truly helps. You need to know what you love to get what you love. Some self-knowledge, self-confidence, self-management, and self-reliance can go a long way toward creating a successful entrepreneurial adventure that you love. Once you've done it, you'll know what I mean.

Chapter 1

How I Broke Free

autonomist n. *somebody who wants or promotes autonomy*

autonomy n. *the condition of being independent; self-governance*

I was standing in the shower before work one day, shifting from dreams to reality, and a sudden flood of relief swept through my entire body and mind. I realized, I can just quit this job that has been weighing me down for more than five years! It was a moment of rare elation. I would simply resign my position. I could give my two-weeks notice and be done with the biggest problem in my life. Also, I could set in motion the chain of events I needed to regain my freedom and start my own business where all of the hassles and headaches I had been dealing with for several years would simply vanish into my past. The moment would be sweet, I imagined. When I stepped out of the shower, I told my wife, Michelle, about my plan. She welcomed the news with open arms. "Good for you. You don't need them. I'm tired of hearing you complain about your job," she said. Those straightforward yet wonderful words boosted my positive glow to create one of the happiest days of my life: The day I quit my last job.

As I pulled up my pants and tied my shoes, I was floating on air. When I sat down at my desk for one of the last times ever, I smiled from ear to ear. Let freedom ring!

Some people say that entrepreneurs are born that way, but I'll leave that debate to those with more scientific minds. When I was born, I had a sister and brother. My mother was a secretary at the local hospital, and my father worked at a nearby steel mill, a job he got after four years in the U.S. Air Force. Neither of my parents ever went to college, but they helped put my siblings and me through the University of Delaware.

Although this book is about how you can quit your job and start your own, the personal story of my roots and who I am plays an integral part in how I think about both business and life: the two elements that will combine more than ever before when you take the plunge into self-employment.

I mention my parents because it is important to recognize the roots from which we sprang. First they paid for my college education, which is still one of the nicest things anyone has ever done for me. The last financial help they ever gave me was money for a Mac Classic II, a computer I used to start my first publishing business in 1992.

Fire Your Boss

After five years of making a living as a self-employed publisher in California, working with a partner, a dozen freelancers, hundreds of advertisers, and a handful of printers and pressmen, my life took a dramatic shift.

On a visit back to Delaware for my ten-year high school reunion, I reconnected with a former girlfriend. We soon turned our long-distance relationship into a new life together in California. Suddenly I was a new husband and the stepfather of two young girls. When the financial limitations of my small business became apparent, I made the responsible decision to take a full-time job as a cameraman and board operator for the local NBC affiliate in Eureka, California. Although I fully intended to keep my magazine, *Anthem Monthly*, in print while I worked for the television station's news department, I was able to publish only one final edition of my magazine before falling into the daily demands of working for somebody else. The upside was that I quickly returned to a career in news reporting that I loved in the exciting medium of television I had only flirted with at the University of Delaware. As more time passed since my last publication, the steady income to support my family lulled me into letting my first business fade away. It was an apathetic end to an exciting and independent time in my life, but it also allowed an even more exciting and satisfying part of my life to unfold. I had learned from *Anthem Monthly* and lived solely from its proceeds for more than six years, but the time had come to move on and get "a real job."

Two-and-a-half years later, my daughter Toby was born. My friends, anchors for the 6 and 11 P.M. news on Channel 3, greeted her arrival on the air from the news desk. One year later, after a successful and satisfying experience as a full-time TV news reporter, chief videographer, and assignment editor, my family and I decided to move back to the East Coast. In a satisfying moment that would reverberate for the rest of my life, I turned in my letter of resignation to a boss I would be happy to live without. "Thank you for the opportunity to work for your organization." My station manager, a unflappable displaced Texan in a northern California town, was kind and understanding, and I never saw him again. With the prospect of a wide-open future filled with family, travel, and adventure, giving my two-weeks notice was satisfying beyond words.

I returned to Delaware exactly one decade after I had left for California in 1990. After some initial searching on the Internet, I had several job offers, including a couple from companies where friends worked. The first job I chose was with a small startup that helped other companies promote their businesses through trade shows. After only a few short months, I realized I had made a big mistake. I was glad to hear that the company whose job I had turned down only couple of months earlier was still hiring. I interviewed with them again and was hired. The day I was offered the position, I wrote and turned in another satisfying resignation letter to my boss at the startup. I was glad to be done with the extremely dull and uninteresting work that dominated my days. The day I sat down at my desk to write that letter, I was giddy with anticipation. When I told my unhappy co-workers that I was quitting, they didn't believe me at first. When they saw my joyful smile and heard the happy tune I was humming, they knew it was no joke. It was the happiest day I ever had at that job.

For the next nearly six years at my new job, I toiled away in my lifeless cubicle, moving up from managing editor to senior editor at a publishing firm that was embroiled in many dire changes. As a privately owned family business that had been passed down through multiple generations, the company's organizational culture was old school. Although I made the most of my time there, making a positive contribution while working with more freelancers, suppliers, and customers, I learned much about the world of business and was able to determine what I did and did not like. Everything I learned during those days increased my ability to eventually strike out on my own. The tiny cubicle in which I worked served as a valuable incubator for the ideas I would eventually use to turn my life around. I developed visions of better work–life balance. I imagined a quiet space where I could be more productive with my time. I envisioned uninterrupted time when I could write and create the work that had meaning to me. When I turned in my letter of resignation from this job, I provided my former employer with a list of prices for my services, which they were happy to use since they had failed to train anyone else to do the work I had been performing for years. The time was right, and I took the opportunity. Now, three years later, I can see that it was the best decision I ever made.

Get with the Times

Once upon a time, in a bygone era, a career followed a linear trajectory. A boss could last you a lifetime. Times have changed, to say the least.

In the twentieth century, an employee could work for the same company for fifty years and then collect a hearty pension at retirement. In the twenty-first century, careers more often are a patchwork of jobs and job types. In a post-Enron era, when the loyalty bonds between companies and employees have hit an all-time low and droop lower daily, an employee needs more security than a naïve trust in a single company to pay the bills for a lifetime. Learning to exploit one's own resources to create a job has become a skill that is more vital now than ever before.

Why would anyone want to start his or her own business? Let me count the ways! One day, when I was twenty-five, I took a risk and quit my cool job at the *SF Weekly*, a big, hip weekly in a big, hip city, to become the publisher of a small monthly magazine in a small, remote northern California town. The decision was based on a variety of factors, but none of them was because I disliked my job.

I had a great job at a great publication. But suddenly, an energetic guy named Guy from Humboldt County, California, sold his monthly magazine, *Edge City*, to my girlfriend, Lara Hammond and me. For a year I had been writing for his magazine while working in San Francisco. Now, a year later, he was telling me he was selling the magazine. Lara and I both loved the idea of being our own bosses, so we quit the *SF Weekly*. We each borrowed a little money from our parents, bought a computer and printer, gave Guy some money, and moved into his old alleyway workplace/living space. We were self-employed publishers overnight.

That was our story, and everybody has his or her own story to tell about what it was like to change directions in life, shift gears, and start up a new path to personal and professional fulfillment. Although Lara and I had some pretty intense conflicts during our four years together as co-publishers, I'm glad we did it and I would not change a thing.

Today, like many other small-business owners, I take what I have learned from my time as a young business owner and apply it to what I do every day in my current job as a self-employed writer and editor. I picked my profession because it was something I could do well and because it makes me happy. From the first time I was paid to meet a deadline with my writing, I knew that I enjoyed this type of work. Nothing satisfies me more than publishing and broadcasting my creative work. Everybody has something they do well that can earn them some money if they put their minds to it.

I know what I like. I have found a profession that fits me like a glove. If you want to put yourself in a self-employment situation, start with something at which you are good. Put your talents to work for you. That's what all of these people in this book did. They found real work that gives them satisfaction, and found a way to do it as a full-time job.

Seek Clues

To find the clues that lead to your best possible future, look at the most positive and productive experiences in your life. If you have preferences, explore them thoroughly with more learning. Put your spare time into Web sites, books, conversations with experts, classes, or work experiences. Get started, but don't do anything rash. The best life changes take a little preparation.

Lara, my first partner, and I spent a week with Guy Cross, the founder of *Edge City*, before we took it over for ourselves. I shadowed him for the final weeks of his last deadline at the magazine. He introduced me to his vast network of writers and advertisers while I learned every aspect of his business. This hands-on immersion into his business built on my own six years in print journalism and Lara's business acumen as the office manager at the *SF Weekly*, a startup itself. By the time Guy drove off to start another paper in New Mexico, we believed we had more than enough skills and experiences to run our own paper. Once we met our first deadline, we knew we were right.

Get More Information

Here are four sources of information that will help you explore how you can work for yourself:

- **Self-knowledge**. Know yourself by looking inward. What makes you happy? What can you truly do well? If you don't know, ask those around you. If you don't know people who can help you clearly evaluate your skills, find some. Take classes to get inside your own head. Determine what it is you love to do. Watch out for passing fancies. Become an expert at something before you rely on your knowledge of that area to pay the bills on time. Make sure you really enjoy the job you pursue. Be truthful with yourself about what work really satisfies you.

- **Customer Knowledge.** Customers are the oxygen that keeps your company breathing. Seek out potential customers wherever they might lurk. Listen closely to potential customers to find out what they need. Ask many questions. Learn ways you can create value for people. Don't trust your instincts until you have some proof to back them up. Devour books, forage through trade magazines, scour Web sites, and learn everything you can about your field and the people who pay for what you want to do to make a living.

- **Competitor Knowledge.** Inquire about other people who do what you want to do. Seek out competitors and find ways to make them your customers. Suppliers can help you learn what you need to know to compete. Make competitors your friends and they might treat you as a resource rather than a threat. Small business owners love to talk about their work, so ask for information. Make friends. Be inquisitive and sincere.

• **Market Knowledge.** Use every resource at your disposal, including books, periodicals, blogs, Web sites, and online communities to develop social networks. Seek social situations with experts in your field. Creating connections within your industry can pay off with referrals and new customer possibilities. Make many phone calls and send numerous e-mails to stretch your network of friends, customers, and other sources of market information. Take notes during your investigation and put what you learn to use.

Nobody knows what the future holds, but if you continue to look over the horizon for ideas about your business and how it can be improved, you will be better prepared for the long haul. There is no such thing as stasis in life. Time keeps chugging on, so ideas that work today can become slowly outdated unless you keep up with the future by building new connections to replace old ones that have run their course. Nothing lasts forever, so hedge your bets by continually pursuing new, more desirable customers and results.

If you don't enjoy the selling aspect of your small business, hire somebody to take that load off your shoulders. If numbers aren't your thing, hire a CPA. If you have legal questions, ask a lawyer. Find people you trust, then let them do their jobs. Don't micromanage your people, but stay on top of their efforts by checking their work. Praise them when it is done well. Teach them when there is room for improvement.

Explore the Latest Technology

Every year humans devise newer and better ways to do work, which can be transformed into self-employment opportunities with the right application. Technology can be part of your product and service designs, or merely the way you distribute your product or service. Although many people make their money from cutting-edge technology, many of the business owners featured here use very little new technology in their businesses. Some have Web sites, others don't. Using a computer and my Windows Office package of software, supplemented with some PhotoShop, Quark, Excel, and AOL skills, I make a living for myself. If I didn't learn these applications on the job somewhere, I took a class to get up to speed. Although some people might see me as technologically savvy, many others could argue that I'm a Neanderthal because I have never shopped on eBay. The younger you are, the more likely you are to have the technological skills that can help you pay the bills.

The latest technology in laptops and portable printers can set you apart from your field of competitors. Independent contractor Joe Kelly says he writes and prints many of his customer proposals on a computer in his pickup truck after assessing a job, allowing him to immediately produce a contract.

Twenty-first-century technology can easily and inexpensively increase efficiency for a small business while producing competitive advantage. Educate yourself on the latest technology in your industry by surfing the Web and talking to anybody who knows anything about the subject you want to explore. More information is always better than less when making a decision, but once you have spent enough time exploring all of your options, make a choice.

If you are ready to buy, take a deep breath. Without spending a dime, take a long, leisurely stroll through your local technology store and take notes on prices and new gadgetry that might help you do your job better. Think about your needs for the future and ways these techno-toys can increase your efficiency and give you an edge. Look across your competitive landscape and imagine how you could improve the work you see others doing. After several trips around physical stores where you can touch and analyze the actual item and quiz personnel about compatibility and cost-effectiveness, go online and price the item and similar options. Then, when it comes time to make your purchase, you are an expert on the item and can make an informed decision. Before pulling out your checkbook, take a quick glance in the yellow pages for a local, small business you can support with the money you have now allotted for the technology you seek. Supporting other small businesses can often produce reciprocal arrangements while producing customers and connections.

Before purchasing software items, look into student discounts and deals. If you are buying a high-priced software package, consider taking a class at your local community college. An inexpensive class can make you a real student. Many online companies give students extraordinary discounts on the products they sell. You will benefit from the training, your company will benefit from the information and the product, and you both will enjoy the savings, which can more than offset the price of the class.

Focus on Sustainability

Low-cost laptops, printers, digital voice recorders, and cameras allow freelance writers and photographers to produce work once only possible with expensive equipment and software. The Internet has helped to save billions of trees and dollars thanks to the conversion of many information processes from paper to digital. Online mail and communication capabilities allow desktop publishers to work in a virtually paper-free environment, practically eliminating the need for expensive paper while saving forests and preventing landfill waste. Creating sustainable business practices, such as recycling cans, water bottles, and any waste materials can save small businesses loads of money, cut overhead, and provide owners and employees with a sense of pride by putting their environmental awareness into action. Reducing waste saves time and money, so address it within your business by taking time to envision ways unused material and time can be better utilized with a long-range plan for a sustainable future.

Looking into your garbage and knowing what gets thrown away can deeply inform you about what's going on around you. For example, tiny scraps of blue ribbon are scattered around my computer. If you are a parent, you probably know why. The small blue satin ribbon scraps are an indication that my daughter has just cut off the ribbon that ties together the tiny plastic envelope containing an Internet password that she needs to play with her new stuffed animal online. Looking at the computer savvy ingrained in the next generation, we catch a glimpse of the endless variation of digital possibilities with which we will be facing the years ahead. Hopefully, we can also teach them to pick up their scraps of tiny blue ribbons when they are done with them.

Many of us, from Generation Xers to Baby Boomers, to Generation Y, are now living with Webkinz-loving Millennials in our daily lives, the first of which will be ready to vote in less than a decade. This generation has connectivity needs that are hard-wired into their ways of life thanks to the millions of ways we have used computers to make them better, faster, stronger. The customer of the future is interconnected with the technology we gave them at birth, so the business owner of the future must become as savvy about the needs of all potential customers to know how to compete and thrive.

Consider the Internet

Hairdresser Rachel Beaupre says she never had a Web site for her business, yet it continues to grow and thrive. Yoga instructor Weese Wagner has had a business Web site for a few years, but she's embarrassed that it doesn't even include her new logo for Yoga U. Frank Holodick only just got his Web site off the ground for his barbershop, many years after his company was well underway, and he's not sure if it has changed anything for his business. Personally, although I neglect the potential of my own Web site, it is there.

Web sites, blogs, podcasts, and so on, make the Internet a great tool for the self-employed. Like many other business owners, I use the Internet every day to connect with what I need to know to do my job as a writer and editor. I would not be self-employed without the benefits of the Internet because desktop publishing software and hardware have improved to the point where they are both affordable and accessible. But my Web site does not bring in the business that pays my bills. That money comes from something that requires no technology: relationships.

LinkedIn, MySpace, Facebook, Blogger, and the like, thrive as excellent networking tools and present vast possibilities for deep relationships. On the other hand, my revenue is a result of the human relationships I have cultivated for many years with face-to-face interactions, phone calls, e-mails, and the hard work I do daily to bring value to my customers through my services. Although technology helps me get my job done with hardware and software I use daily, the relationship-building that earns me checks comes from daily interaction with the people who know they can count on me to give them the quality work they require. This includes responding to their e-mails and phone calls on a daily basis, reacting to emergencies effectively, setting the right tone in meetings, and being somebody with whom somebody else wants to work. None of these involves technology more intricate than a telephone and an e-mail address I monitor every day.

Small-business owners have to decide what new technology will be the right fit for growing their own specific business. When considering cost, patience is key because the price of technology is dropping in many different ways, such as the giant drop in the price of a hard drive or an iPhone, and trends come and go. Many people have spent thousands of dollars on the latest technology only to discover that it really isn't the key to their business they imagined. When it comes to the complexities of technology, simplicity is often the answer. Knowing yourself and knowing your customers are things technology can help you do, but there are other ways, including working together face to face, talking over the phone, and even spending time together away from work.

Nurture Positive Relationships

When I started my second business three years ago, I knew exactly what I could do to earn a living by looking at the business situation in the company where I was working at the time. From inside the physical and organizational structure of the company I could see that the firm was ready for a shift to outsourcing, so I allowed that change to happen by quitting, and then offering the company my services at an hourly or project rate as a private contractor rather than an employee. I created value for my former employer by offering them increased flexibility and saving them thousands of dollars in employee costs. A positive relationship with my boss allowed me to keep working with the company as an independent subcontractor instead of an employee. With a handful of other customers and potential customers already in the works, I took a chance and made a change. My relationship with my former employer remains strong, as we continue to work together on many very satisfying projects, including my first book, *The Management Gurus*. Mutually beneficial relationships like this can help you get a business up and running. Look around yourself for similar scenarios. The following chapters offer a number of ways to turn positive relationships into business opportunities.

Top Takeaways

1. Fire your boss. Sometimes we get stuck in the wrong job, or we outgrow a job. If your current work situation is unhealthy, mentally or physically, get out. Create an alternative financial situation and give your boss the boot before somebody gets hurt.

2. Get with the times. Books, Web sites, blogs, podcasts, newspapers, and magazines give us super powers if we pay close attention. Classes make us even more powerful. Hands-on experience is the best way to move your dream of self-employment forward.

3. Seek clues. Go to experts for advice. Act like a reporter: Ask a million questions.

4. Get more information. Take time to find out more about your customers, your market, your competitors, and yourself. Look inward, outward, and forward for a niche that will sustain you better than you currently have it where you are working now.

5. Explore the latest technology. Whether you need it or not, it's good to know what's out there. Take some time to get to know the latest technological trends. This might require stepping out of your comfort zone. Younger people can help you learn.

6. Focus on sustainability. Find ways to work where nothing is wasted. Look at the long-term effects of every purchase, including packaging and energy use.

7. Consider the Internet. Maybe you need it, or maybe you don't, but every business owner should make an informed decision about whether he or she needs a Web presence.

8. Nurture positive relationships. Don't burn your bridges. Look at everyone, including your old boss, as a potential customer or source of referrals.

Chapter 2

What Are You Going to Do with the Rest of Your Life?

aplomb n. *self-assurance*

Derek Green's press release is impressive:

> *Since his earliest memories, Derek Green has held the vision to design women's clothing and manage his own company. All the steps he has taken, from his education at Parsons to his tenure as head designer for [a top global fashion company], have been made with this singular purpose. Each position has given him the opportunity to learn and perfect something new. On Sept. 12, 2005, Derek presented his first runway collection at New York's Olympus Fashion Week and his designs are currently sold at 300 stores, including Fred Segal and New York–based Atrium. He now produces ten collections a year for hundreds of retailers like Fred Segal, Saks Fifth Avenue and Nordstrom's. His latest retro-inspired collection—velvet suits, coats, and jackets with fur-lined collars, and menswear-inspired fabrics—is priced from $100 to $600.*

DEREK GREEN, 40—NEW YORK FASHION DESIGNER

Today, Derek is a successful fashion designer who lives in New York City with his wife and three children. After college, he started his professional career at one of the fastest-growing fashion companies at the time. Next, he took a better job at another top company in the fashion industry, jumping at the opportunity to move his career in yet another direction. Eight years later, Derek resigned from an enviable job to start his own fashion label. Today, women all around the world, including top models, celebrities, and everyday folks, wear his designs. Thanks to Derek's hard work building a solid reputation in the industry, as well as a recent contract with a major clothing distributor, the Derek Green brand has grown by leaps and bounds since its inception.

When Derek resigned from his position at one of the biggest names in the fashion industry in 2001 to start a clothing company bearing his own name, he says the decision to resign was difficult, but he did it because he had to follow his dreams. While growing up in suburban Baltimore County in Maryland, Derek says he wanted to be a fashion designer for as long as he can remember:

> It first started with wanting to be an artist. I really wanted to be an artist because I did well at drawing. My teacher loved the way I would draw, and said, "Well, you're going to be an artist." Then, when I found out that artists don't really make a living, I thought, I don't want to do that one. I wanted to have a family one day, and I didn't want to be dead once I started making any money. At that point, I always liked clothes, and I discovered fashion. By the time I was thirteen, all I wanted to do was grow up and go to New York to become a fashion designer. My father was like, "No, what do you *really* want to do?"
>
> And I said, "*That*'s what I really want to do."

Derek's father was a longshoreman who wanted his son to go to college to become a doctor or lawyer or to choose another profession with a financially sound future. Derek says, "It wasn't a bad plan, but it just wasn't where my heart was."

When Derek was born, his mother was a surgical nurse. By the time Derek was two years old, she decided to stay home to take care of Derek and his brothers and sister. His mother encouraged Derek to follow his dreams, while his father urged him to be practical and find a job that would allow him to support a family some day.

When he was thirteen, Derek told his parents he wanted to go to New York to be a fashion designer. He says that despite his mother's fears that New York City would "eat her baby alive," and his father's insistence that he learn how to make a comfortable living for himself and his future family, his dream prevailed.

Keep At It

Derek persisted. "I just kept at it," he says. "I kept saying I wanted to do that. Any class or anything I could take about sewing or drawing, I would do it." A year before he was ready to graduate, his parents were still adamant that he wait longer to move to New York City. But his father was warming to his dream of becoming a fashion designer:

> My dad was always the type of person that, you show him, he'll get behind you. There was a huge fashion show in Maryland, and I submitted my stuff. I had seventy-four garments that I was sewing myself, and I had a friend coming over and fitting them. My dad comes down and he sees me doing that. My stuff is all over the floor, here and there. Well, he went up and told my mother, "Rent that boy a rolling rack." That was the last time I heard any fight about wanting to be a designer because, to him, it had proved that I was going to do the work to make it work.

Although they supported his career choice, they still were not ready for their son to move to New York City. They wanted him to stay in a more livable city, so Derek compromised by choosing Philadelphia. Fashion illustration classes at the Art Institute of Philadelphia taught him many of the skills he still uses today in his business, but New York was never far from his mind, so he took his associate's degree and portfolio and was admitted to Parsons in New York. Shortly before he left for New York, he met his future wife at the Art Institute. She was also pursuing a career in fashion after medical school did not meet her expectations. She also wanted to live in New York, so she and Derek moved to New York City together.

At the time, Derek's idol was renowned fashion designer Marc Jacobs. Derek explains:

> I saw [TV news magazine] *48 Hours* when I was in high school. Marc Jacobs said that Perry Ellis was his idol, and Ellis told him that if he wanted to be a fashion designer he had to move to New York and go to Parsons, so I was sold. To me, it was the end-all. I thought, if Perry Ellis told him that and look where he is, that's what I'm doing. I was able to transfer my credits toward a bachelor's degree at Parsons. I actually did three years at Parsons and two years in Philadelphia. I got to work with such great people. That was one of the great things about Parsons, especially in that day, is that they would break the kids up into groups of five, because there weren't big classes, and they would put you with a mentor. I got to work with Marc Jacobs, which was amazing. I got to work with Calvin Klein. I got to work with Michael Kors. You would do these capsules with these mentors, and then you would put on a fashion show. It was amazing.

Share Your Dreams with Others

Suddenly, he was working with top fashion designer Marc Jacobs, who was one of the role models Derek had always wanted to emulate by becoming a New York fashion designer. Jacobs and Derek worked together on a line of clothing for Perry Ellis.

The dreams he imagined as a teenager had come true. Soon he was working with fashion luminary Michael Kors. Derek's wife Sheri helped make this connection happen because she was doing public relations work for Kors. Derek began to make a name for himself and his talents as a New York City designer while working on fashion shows with Kors and then Calvin Klein. He says his time working with Calvin Klein helped him gain a better perspective of the fashion industry.

Set Great Goals

While working with top luminaries in the fashion world, who each had his own thriving design firm, Derek developed a new career goal that he would eventually reach with only a few more years of patience and persistence: He decided he wanted to start his own business, but not yet.

Working hard at school and on the runway, and mentored by the best designers in the business, Derek was sowing the seeds of his future business. But his dreams needed more than a great education and grand ambitions to take root, so he sought a job in the corporate world in which he could learn about the fashion industry beyond the "glitz and glam" of New York City's Seventh Avenue.

Derek decided to seek a corporate job. Although many of his friends were already graduating and beginning to work for large companies such as Gap and Banana Republic, they complained of feeling as if they were shoved in a corner cubicle. Derek dreamed of a more satisfying career move.

Shortly after graduating from Parsons, Derek was hired by a large, big-name clothing company. Executives at the men's clothing company were looking for a designer who could help them transition into women's clothing. Derek was hired as part of a five-person team to help build the company's women's division. His work experience in the corporate realm helped him learn about the fashion industry from another vantage point.

While working with the fashion industry's top talent at school, Derek enjoyed the glamorous, hands-on, fast-paced environment of New York's Seventh Avenue. After so much excitement in his early career, he dreaded finding himself in a boring job:

> When I went to the corporate world, I really didn't want to get involved with somewhere where I was like a drone, just going along, so I always tried to look for startups. [The company] was starting up. It was a fledgling at that point. There was no women's team. The men's division was doing well, and it was great. It was a great experience. I got to travel. I got to experience things as a startup team that I wouldn't have if I had gone into a ready-made system. So that was really good.

Derek spent the next five years learning everything he could from his dream job in New York City as a designer at one of the world's top clothing companies.

Get Experienced

After five years in the industry, Derek was ready for a job change, so he took a job at a big-name men's fashion company that was starting its first women's division. For the next four years, he rounded out his corporate experience working his way up in a different company with its own unique processes and systems. Four years later, after almost a decade of working for other people, Derek reached a crossroads in his work. His career was moving along swimmingly thanks to increasing management responsibilities and more money. On the other hand, he was ready for more independence. "At that point, I was either going to start buying houses and things like that, and have to afford my life, and keep affording my life, and staying a slave to that, or take the money that I had saved up and start my own [business]."

Derek says the decision to resign was not an easy one. One factor that helped him make the break from his job was a conflict with his manager, which was making him very unhappy at work. He was ready for a change.

At the end of 2000, Derek struggled with his job options. Although he was making great money at his current job, he also had dreams of starting his own clothing line. In addition, he had two children, and another on the way.

After years of education and experience, months of preparation, and daily conversations with his wife and family members about his plan to start his own business, Derek resigned from his job in spring 2001. He says, "It was one of those forks in the road where it was like, if you stay here, are you going to grow, or are you going to bite the bullet and go out on your own?"

There is really no easy way to make the leap into self-employment. Every entrepreneur faces the decision to change course by weighing all of the factors involved in his or her life and career. Careful examination of the financial and familial realities is vital. Sometimes the most difficult struggles lead to the greatest breakthroughs, but good advice can help to guide the decision. Faced with one of the biggest decisions of his life, Derek sought council. He says, "I remember talking to everyone who I trusted their opinion, and trying to figure out an easy way to do it. Is it best to do it on the side a little bit? Maybe I should do this. Maybe I should do that."

With a pregnant wife and two children at home, Derek admits that he wondered whether starting his own business was a "selfish dream." Resigning from his well-paying job was a very difficult decision.

One day, his decision to leave became very clear. At a meeting with his new direct manager, a discussion about problems at work turned into a shouting match. Accusations began to fly. Before the yelling could continue, Derek says he walked out of the room and slammed the door behind him. His relationship with his new boss had become toxic over the past several months. Suddenly, Derek knew that leaving his job and starting his own business was the right thing to do. He says his mind was made up. That day, he went home and thought deeply about his next step.

> I have to do this. If I don't, it will be something that I'll always regret. And this is the perfect opportunity where I'm not being forced out. I'm not being asked to leave. I can leave, and I have good reasons to leave, and I don't have to feel bad about it.

Recognize the Moment

Derek says there was a moment when his decision to leave became apparent.

> All of us feel it. When you're working and it gets past the point that "this is fun" or "this is adventurous" and it just becomes monotonous. It becomes an "I can't believe this is going to be the rest of my life!" sort of feeling.

Derek says it took about three months before he realized how unhappy he had become in his job for a large company. His boss gave him a solid reason to leave. Because he didn't want to risk falling into a similar role in another corporate job, he decided to pursue his dream of starting his own fashion company.

When he left his job, he received a severance package of four months' salary. With that money, the additional cash he had saved, and help from family members, he started Derek Green Designs.

Jump in the Deep End

Derek says it is difficult to describe the feeling of starting a business:

> There is no other way I can describe it other than just holding your breath and jumping in the deep end and figuring out how to swim. I truly believe that if you know too much about what's coming after you start your own [business], you probably wouldn't do it. It's almost like ignorance is bliss. You jump in there and start kicking and swimming, and you go for the best. If you knew what was coming, if you knew that when you jumped in the deep end you're going to eventually swim, but you're going to swallow a lot of water, your nose is going to burn, but you'll make it to the edge, you probably wouldn't do it as quickly as if you just jumped in and didn't know what was going to happen. It's almost like feeling the water before you get in. You know how cold it is.

Don't Believe Everything You Hear

Before turning in his letter of resignation, Derek had already begun to work on his game plan for starting his own business. For years he had been establishing the many solid connections he would need to start his own independent fashion design company. The path to independence was taking shape. "I had already talked to different production houses that could produce my line." When he quit, he tapped into many of the relationships he had nurtured while working for big companies.

Although some of his plans worked out, Derek says that many of the connections he was relying on to help him start his business were unavailable when he needed them. Although many smaller companies followed through on their promises, Derek says some of the larger companies were less interested in working with him when he no longer had the big dollars of a large corporation behind him. He says it was harder than he thought to find manufacturers willing to produce his smaller clothing runs.

Derek explains that another big eye-opener for him about the nature of self-employment was the number of hours that his new business required for sales and production management. He says, "During the day I was making sure the payroll was going to be paid, making sure the delivery was going to happen, making sure that the relationship with the stores was going to happen. That was what I had to do during the hours that everybody else was working." To do all the necessary work, he learned to push the part of his business that he enjoyed, such as designing clothes, to long late-night sessions at his drawing table while his family slept.

Derek says that it was much harder to get his business off the ground than he thought it would be. He also says that although over the years he has watched many of his friends who stayed in the corporate world enjoy lavish paychecks and vacations, he wouldn't trade his experiences as an independent designer for any of it. "If I think about who I was before I started my own [business] and who I am today, I like me much better than if I had just stayed in the corporate world like a lot of my friends." Derek says there are many other differences between his lifestyle now and his life working for a large corporation. "When you work in the fashion industry, even if you go from job to job, your stocks follow you, and all those things, and having a great paycheck really works out. With having your own [business], some months are great and you're like, 'Hey, we're in the money!' and some months you have to ride it out until the next month."

Listen to Those with Experience

In addition to his family, bosses, and teachers, other people in Derek's life have taught him valuable lessons about surviving the struggles of business ownership. He says he always keeps in mind the story of a friend who started a company from nothing and grew it to a multimillion dollar chain of international stores. He says she was recently forced to resign from her own company after being squeezed out by unscrupulous partners. She is now suing to regain control of the company she started. Derek remembers this whenever making deals with new partners. He also knows that although self-employment can be a roller-coaster ride with many twists and turns, keeping your expectations realistic can prevent you from being disappointed. Derek says, "I guess, if you do it for riches, that's not always going to happen. There's always going to be ups and downs with your business—even Donald Trump [has them]—there's always going to be good times and bad times."

Derek says he also believes that a business owner is the type of person who needs to be independent. "I think the person who needs to work for him or herself is someone who, first of all, does not like to be told what to do, especially if you think you are doing it the right way. You don't want to be under people who are jealous or people who just try to stamp out your light."

By having his own business, Derek says he is able to better live by his own ideals and values, even when doing so is difficult:

> One of the things I promised myself once I started my own company was that I was not going to work with people whom I didn't want to work with. I was just not going to do it. I don't care how much money. How many times do you have to work with people during the day where you think, I would not even talk to this person because of the negative energy coming from them, let alone work with them? I just promised myself that I wouldn't do that. It's a choice. It's not an easy choice.

Make a Choice

But Derek says that the difficulties of self-employment are worth the struggles thanks to the many positive changes it brings to life. "Personally, it has improved my relationship with my wife and my kids because I have no one telling me when I can spend time with them and when I can't spend time with them," he says.

> If I want to take a day and spend the time with Sheri because I feel like we need it, I'll take a day and spend time with Sheri. I'll just do that work at night or I'll do it on the weekend. I know my workloads, and I know what I need to do. I don't need someone standing over me who is being paid to say, "You have to be here from nine until this hour because I have to make sure you are doing your job."

Derek says, for him, it is all about making a choice.

It's my choice if I'm going to be at the PTA meeting or be at a play, because it's my choice. It's not someone else saying, "Well, you know, you've taken off this much time. I really don't want you to go." If I want to go to the beach with Sheri and her family for that week, it's my choice. I like that feeling. I like that feeling of being in control of my schedule and how I do things.

Be Confident

Derek says starting his own business has profoundly changed his outlook on life. Self-confidence was one big dividend.

I think you build this confidence about yourself of like, "I *can* handle it!" I think that was a big confidence booster. Not to have a huge team of people behind me, and the name. There was a point where if I went somewhere and I said, "Oh yeah, I'm a designer for [a well-known firm]," the seas would part. You sort of become who you work for.

He found it gratifying to make the transition from getting recognition for representing somebody else to being recognized for his own hard work. "Also, it was just the point of having a dream as a kid and actually not standing back and just having a dream, but actually going for it. That builds a lot of confidence in a person. Even if it doesn't work, it's like, 'Well, at least I got off my ass and tried. I didn't do what most people do and just talk about it.'"

Fix Mistakes

Like many entrepreneurs, Derek says, "Other than marrying my wife, [starting a business] was the best decision I ever made in my life, definitely."

He adds that he tries to learn from his successes and mistakes.

I would say the best times that I've learned are when I've made mistakes and I had to fix them. I learned the most in those situations. When I did it right, I moved on to the next thing. When I made a mistake and it had to be resolved, that's when I've learned the most. I have to be honest, if I didn't have my pitfalls, I wouldn't be where I am right now. When I do have a failure and something doesn't work out, I try to look at it as, what lesson did I learn from it? If I learned a lesson from it, then I was supposed to learn that lesson, and I'll move on.

As Wal-Mart and other big-box stores fill the country with inexpensive goods from outside the United States, Derek points out that his original dreams of being a designer have changed as the world has changed. As his wife Sheri puts it, "You have to be like water going around a rock when you have your own company." Derek adds:

You really do, because you might have your plan, and have it set up this way, but trust me, there's going to be at least ten roadblocks if not walls in your way. You have to sort of maneuver your way around. With the economy doing so bad, business is changing. There used to be hundreds of specialty stores that sold small designer lines. Everything now is being pulled into this big corporate production. You've got Costco. They buy things in bulk, so the price is driven down. There used to be a time when you went shopping and if you didn't go to a small boutique, you had to go to Gap or Banana Republic for stuff that is very "bulk" looking. Now, you have H&M and Forever 21 and places where you can get designer looks right after they show them but at a quarter of the price. So, you've got to figure out a new way of doing business.

To change with the times, Derek says he spent time rethinking his business. "One of the things that I had to do was try to think out of the box. I didn't even think of QVC, but my partner was the one who said, 'I want to take this stuff to QVC because I really think there is a business for it there.'"

Be Open to New Directions

Although he didn't think QVC would be interested in helping him market his clothing line, the company offered him a contract to appear on its international TV shopping network. QVC was interested in selling the kinds of fashions that Derek creates. Derek says this new direction was unexpected, but he welcomed it. "Did I ever think I would be on QVC? Was that in my vision at all? No. But they paid great and it worked out."

While keeping his larger dreams and goals in mind, Derek modified his business so he could survive and thrive. Part of that modification was seeking a business partner to help his business get off the ground during its early years. The partner he found was a young man from a wealthy family who wanted to break into the fashion industry. Derek says, "He was basically looking for something to branch out into. He was looking for a new opportunity." Derek's company had the product; his partner had the money. The partner's half of the business consisted of making sure products shipped on time and keeping track of production costs and financing. The partnership worked for a while, but things changed after one year. When the partner said he wanted to limit his investment and the company's growth, Derek sought another partner. "I'm not going to turn business away because my financers can't finance it, so I had to find another partner." After buying back his partner's share of the business, Derek hooked up with a new team of partners. He says, "That didn't work out too well because they basically tried to take over and do one of those situations like what happened to my other friend, and sort of squeeze Sheri and me out, and take over the business. I was like, 'To hell with that.'" Since then, Derek's company has found a better partner who is helping it grow into new areas.

Discover Your Own Needs

Derek says that starting his own business has taught him many new things about himself. For example, he always imagined himself as an easy-going person and has now learned that he's actually a perfectionist. He says, "When it comes to my own company and what I want it to represent, to me, that's me representing myself, and it has to be perfect. It has to be done the way it should be done, even if it takes a little more time."

He also learned that he has a hard time asking for help, which resulted in too much stress. "You really can't do it all," he says:

> As you make your money, you have to start hiring people who are good at what you're weak at. It's really hard to admit that you have a weakness because you're supposed

to have all the answers because you're in charge. You're the boss. You're supposed to have all the answers, but you have to surround yourself with the people who can do the things you can't do. Even if it's small: measuring. If you're not that great at measuring, you find people who are when you have the money to hire them and pay them what they are worth.

Value Key Employees

Sometimes the entrepreneurial spirit in a startup can be contagious, to the dismay of the startup's owner. One of Derek's employees became so good at her job that she wanted to break free and start her own business. Although he lost one of his best employees to the entrepreneurial bug, he understands completely. "After two or three years working with me, she decided she really wanted to start her own pattern-making company." Although it was hard to lose her, Derek did not want to stand in her way. He knew that she simply needed to take the same kind of chance he did. He adds, "She's doing really well. It's hard when you get someone you do depend on and then they do leave."

Derek explains that the fact that she was starting her own business helped to ease the pain of her loss. "She said she wouldn't have gotten the chance without my mentoring," he says. But he knows firsthand that a self-employment opportunity is hard to ignore, so today he gets satisfaction knowing he helps his employees find their own opportunities.

Take Charge of Your Destiny

Independence feels natural to self-employed people. Derek says:

> You're supposed to be in charge of your own life. That's the way the American dream was taught to us. You're supposed to be in charge of your destiny. That's what you're told at a very young age.

The entrepreneur is also willing to take risks that many other people won't. In today's changing world, where the loyalty bonds between employer and employee have eroded beyond recognition, it seems as if working for oneself is far less risky than it once was when a better relationship was at stake. Some might even say it is more risky to stay with a company that could abandon its employees at a moment's notice, such as what happened to the employees at Enron, who lost both their jobs and their retirement funds in one fell swoop. Every day, it seems as though pursuing one's own destiny through self-employment is becoming a less risky choice.

Be the Boss You Would Want to Have

One of the choices an employer makes these days is whether or not to test employees for illegal substances. Although many people find this type of screening an infringement on their civil rights, especially in a country that prides itself on freedom from unwarranted searches and seizures, the practice continues to take place throughout many industries. Although most large organizations require some kind of pre-employment "health" screening, which might require a urine sample, many smaller organizations choose to skip the expense of these types of controversial practices.

As an entrepreneur, you will need to consider whether it is cost-effective to pay for drug tests for your employees. Keep in mind all safety and health considerations for your customers. Remember, you will be choosing whether to limit yourself to a smaller pool of employees if you choose to test applicants. Some entrepreneurs have made it a competitive strategy to save operating costs by eliminating these types of expensive and invasive practices for their employees. Hiring employees who value their freedom as much as you value your own can sometimes result in scoring talented individuals who are willing to earn less to share your company's values.

When he was an employee for a large design firm, Derek says he was subjected to random drug tests. He says, "One of the funny things people said was, 'That's why you become a designer so you can do drugs with other designers.'"

Derek said the ramifications of the drug test were severe. If an employee's urine sample tested positive for an illegal substance, he or she was fired. Derek says he disagreed with the policy. "I can understand if I'm walking in here stoned, falling all over the place. Then you'll fire me because I'm not doing my job. But you don't random drug test me."

Standing by his convictions, Derek has no drug-testing policy for his company's employees. Derek says drug testing is too Orwellian for him. "That whole Big Brother thing does not work for me."

Be the Right Type

Derek says starting a business is not for everyone. He believes there is a certain type of person who can't resist starting his or her own business, who can't stop trying to make it on his or her own. Although he says he is one of these people, it doesn't make him better than anyone else. "Just because I'm an entrepreneur doesn't make me any better than someone who's working in a corporate office sitting in a cubicle. It just makes me different. Some people have blonde hair; some people have brown hair."

When seeking advice about new ventures, Derek says he often discusses his plans with his brother-in-law, a top legal counsel for a large media corporation, who adamantly warned him against starting his own business. This is not unusual and entrepreneurs should expect to encounter pessimists, as some people resist risk and change. These are not the people who should be sought out for advice. Choose wisely those from whom you take advice. Contemplate the opinions of the people you trust the most, but make your own decision once you have mulled over all of the best information and ideas. Sleep on it, maybe a few times; then act.

When seeking advice from his friends and family members, Derek says his mother, sister, and wife always tell him to follow his heart, whereas other family members urge him to follow a much more cautious path. He says he always seeks counsel from both sides:

> You need those different opinions around you; a family that you trust and talk to. You know they're only going to be looking out for you. They're telling you what they think is best for you, but you also have to make the decision of what's best for you.

When starting out, Derek says that even though he anticipated the advice from his brother-in-law who warned him not to start his own business, he still wanted to discuss the issue with him. He says, "I like debates, and I wanted to hear his arguments, and see if his arguments were valid. I wanted to hear it." After hearing a list of reasons why he should stay in his current job, including the fact that it was a terrific company, with great benefits and career potential, Derek made his own decision about his career. "I listened. That wasn't the road that I wanted to take, but I wanted to hear that opinion."

Debate and conversation inform a business owner so he or she can make better decisions. Strengths in the area of conversation and communication are essential to a new business owner. Derek's interest in other people's opinions helps him in his work in many other ways as well. "Even with people who work for me, I love getting two people with opposite opinions—can it be done this way or can it be done that way—and then forming my own decision." He adds, "You get opinions; then you do with it what you want to do with it."

Put Family First

Family comes first for most entrepreneurs. The main goal Derek has for his business is to ensure his family is happy and healthy, and hopefully as well off or better off than the family he shared with his own parents. He says his wife has always helped him follow his dreams. He explains, "She's always been supportive, 'Follow your heart, we'll deal with it.'" With the support of Sheri, who also works in the fashion industry for him and others, Derek and his business have been able to help support her and their three children.

A supportive partner, whether a spouse or a close relation who has your best interests in mind, is essential to a positive self-employment experience for almost every entrepreneur. Derek says his wife helps his free spirit make more realistic decisions. He says she provides the crucial counterpoint to his dreams of going out and conquering the world while taking no prisoners. He says his dreams of independence could not have been realized without the solid foundation of her support. "Sheri came along and grounded me a little." He says her rational side helps to balance his creative side, which helps him achieve business success.

Top Takeaways

1. Keep at it. It takes a while to get good at anything, but regular practice can help anyone improve.

2. Share your dreams with others. Doing anything important starts with hearing yourself tell other people about your vision. When you say something good, write it down to capture it. Then keep it growing in your daily routine.

3. Set great goals. Don't settle for mediocre dreams; they won't satisfy you when you reach them. Dream audaciously. It could be the start of something very big and satisfying. Modifying your dreams to fit into reality can make them happen.

4. Get experienced. Learn from the best people who are involved in your dream industry.

5. Recognize the moment. Don't wait until it's too late. Set a clear plan for a healthier work life and execute it with passion and aplomb.

6. Jump in the deep end. At some point you have to make a move or move aside. This is the difference between endlessly talking about doing something and actually doing it.

7. Don't believe everything you hear. Be ready for a few disappointments on the way. Keep a backup plan in the wings to help you ride through rough waters.

8. Listen to those with experience. Listening to stories from those in your industry can help you make more informed decisions.

9. Make a choice. Step up to self-directed work by managing yourself and your time well. Use your time to strengthen your most important relationships.

10. Be confident. Take time to appreciate your successes. Be proud of yourself for trying to live your vision. Don't let mistakes cloud your view of your accomplishments.

11. Fix mistakes. Repeat customers are a business's best friends. Bring people back by taking responsibility for your work.

12. Be open to new directions. Sometimes a partner can help you succeed better than you can alone. Other times a different partner might be a better fit for your business. Improving innovation requires trying new approaches.

13. Discover your own needs. Staying informed about yourself and your business prevents stress. Reassess your needs and priorities to fit new information and changes.

14. Value key employees. Mentor your employees. Take pride in their accomplishments. Treat your people like you wish you had been treated at your previous job.

15. Take charge of your destiny. Don't wait for somebody else to tell you who you should be. Set your own goals and take only the risks you can really afford.

16. Be the boss you would want to have. Part of the joy and independence of owning your own business is showing others how it can be done. Your success is the best demonstration of the benefits of your own personal values, mission, and ethics.

17. Be the right type. Some people are not cut out for the stress and flexibility of self-employment. If you are a worse boss than the boss where you quit, get your old job back.

18. Put family first. Keep your priorities straight. Take care of your most important people first.

Chapter 3

What Will You Do When You Quit?

serendipity n, *the ability to create lucky opportunities from accidents*

Selling a product is one way to make the money you need to be self-sufficient, but providing a service is the foundation of increasingly more entrepreneurial ventures. Although technology has allowed us to do away with many of the tasks that once occupied our lives, one service that has never been replaced is the cutting of hair. Relying on that sense of security, Frank Holodick became a barber, like his father, who would become his boss for more than a decade.

FRANK HOLODICK, 42—BARBERSHOP OWNER

Frank started his business four years ago, but he did more than quit his job. He actually created a new version of the job he had been doing for many years, reorganized and revamped it to suit his growing family's needs, and opened up a new shop of his own to help support his wife Theresa and their two young boys.

Frank's business began when he bought a building in the center of the tiny town of Bellefonte, Delaware, a suburb several miles north of Wilmington, the largest city in the diminutive state.

Out of respect for his father, Michael, Frank named the business after him by calling it Michael's Bellefonte Barber Shop. By dedicating his business to his father, he showed respect to the man who started his own barbershop thirty-two years before. That was the barbershop that helped to raise Frank. He even hired his father as one of his employees. Today, father and son still work side by side, some days talking endlessly, other days hardly saying more than a friendly hello and goodbye. The warm old-fashioned barbershop atmosphere created by these two professionals in their industry has created a loyal following of customers that has kept the Holodicks working independently for nearly four decades.

Like many entrepreneurs, Frank started his business by taking the best parts of his former job at his father's shop and transforming them into a better business that he could make even more successful than the previous one. He says this strategy of transformation has made him more secure, happy, and successful than he has ever been.

Find a Mentor

Frank says he learned much of the job he performs every day from his father.

During the many years of working with his father in a different location, Frank developed many ideas about starting a more profitable barbershop of his own that would be much different than the one his father started in the 1970s. When he decided to start his own business, he hoped his father would join him at the new shop as an employee, but he was wasn't sure what his father would say. Frank explains:

> I hoped he would come, because the situation he was in there wasn't good. He was paying a lot of rent, and it was going up every year. That's what I didn't like about where he was. It was great for a long time, but the last seven years or so, it was getting tougher and tougher.

Closely Consider Owning Versus Leasing

Frank says he saw the writing on the wall. His biggest concern was that the owner of the building where his father's barbershop was located would either knock it down and build something else, or sell it. Although his father had a lease for the space, Frank was concerned about the future. "For many, many years, he signed one-year leases. And then, at the end, he signed a five-year lease." This turn of events complicated Frank's plans to start his own shop, but he persevered.

When Frank bought a different building for his new barbershop, his father still had two-and-a-half years left on the lease for his own location. Frank says, "I called the landlord and told him I bought this building." The Holodicks gave his landlord nine months notice before they planned to leave the space his father had been renting for decades. Although the landlord assured Frank that he would find somebody to fill the vacancy, six months later, no new tenant had been found. The landlord said he would allow Frank to sublease the building, but he provided a long list of business types that he would not allow in order to prevent competition with his other tenants. Frank brought the landlord a dozen possible tenants, but the landlord refused each one. When Frank took out the mortgage on his new shop in June, he was suddenly left paying the mortgage on his new place and the rent on his father's now vacant storefront. Four financially tight months went by before the landlord finally approved a tenant. From October to the end of the lease, the new tenant paid the rent. When the lease ran out, Frank's worries substantially decreased.

The increased overhead was a burden for his new business, but Frank points out that the financial difficulties could have been much worse:

> I had an advantage from Day 1: We were busy. In my original business plan, I was hoping we could bring 70 or 75 percent of the customers [from the old business]. That's what I was hoping for. My goal was, within two years, to have every-thing back to where we were. Take a step back, but within two years, build it back up. And from Day 1, we didn't lose a thing. That helped a lot.

Pay Attention to Your Startup Costs

Although in many ways his business plan is working better than he expected, Frank cannot imagine starting a business from scratch. "It's tough, and I have a lot more respect for anybody who opens a business now that I have one." He adds that starting with a large base of regular customers from the beginning made his life much easier. Facing costs associated with his mortgage, renovation loans, and rent at the old shop, Frank says customer loyalty helped him to survive.

To offset some of his startup costs, Frank used the chairs from his father's old barbershop. But he had to pay for almost everything else. To save cash, he shopped on eBay to find the perfect finishing touch to the barbershop of his dreams: an old-fashioned wooden barbershop bar back to set the tone he sought for his new business. After searching all around the area for months, he found what he was looking for on eBay. A barbershop in Philadelphia was selling just the item. Once he purchased it, he drove up to the city, dismantled the wooden structure piece by piece, numbered each piece, bubble-wrapped everything, drove back to Delaware, and had it reassembled by the men performing his renovations.

Although startup costs were his biggest concern during the months preceding his grand opening, they were relatively low compared with many other types of storefront operations because a barbershop has much less inventory and technology than other new businesses. In other words, the "face value" of a barbershop is relatively low. By using some of his father's old equipment, Frank was able to lower his startup costs while also getting value out of equipment that can be difficult to sell.

While Frank continues to get value from his father's former customers and classic barber chairs, he also entered his business with a clear view of its worth on the market. He learned this firsthand when he put his father's business at its old location on the market. Despite its solid base of clients, his father's business was impossible to sell. Frank explains:

> We were keeping four barbers busy, supporting four families—a very, very successful business—and it's not worth anything, because for somebody who wants to open up a barbershop, it doesn't cost that much to buy the chairs. If

you were going to rent a place, you can find old barber chairs for $500. So, if you have a two-man shop, something like that, you could open up for $5,000!

Develop a Vision

Rather than open his business as a bare-bones enterprise, Frank had a vision. He wanted his place to look and feel like an old-fashioned barbershop. To bring this dream to life, he spent several months and much money adding the finishing touches that make his shop a destination where clients can relax, enjoy a haircut, have a snack and beverage, and share good company. To make his vision a reality, he searched far and wide for the pieces of old barbershops, including the antique barbershop back bar. By creating a distinctive look, Frank was setting a specific tone for his barbershop, which would be different than his father's 1960s-style shop.

In addition, Frank did extensive research to find the right design. On a road trip to Maine with his wife, he stopped by every barbershop he could find, went inside to look around, and talked to the barbers. At one shop, he learned an important lesson about lighting. In the high-end barbershop, Frank noticed some attractive and expensive spotlights that were not being used. When he asked about them, he was told that the owner didn't like to use them because they heated the place up to an unbearable 90 degrees when they were turned on. Frank stored this information in his brain; that's the kind of intelligence you get only from experience or the kind of research he was doing.

Frank says some barbers were reluctant to reveal their secrets. "They're not real sure if you're going to open up on the next block. Once they heard I'm in Delaware, they opened up."

Make Time for Complications

Cutting hair is a common business for independent entrepreneurs as well as franchisees, thanks to the recent proliferation of barbershop franchises such as Supercuts and Pro-Cuts. In contrast, Frank wanted his business to have a unique look and feel, so he did research on the Internet. With so many old-fashioned barbers maintaining their own Web sites, information was easy to find.

For three months, while working full time in his father's barbershop, Frank prepared the new building and the financing to purchase it. He says it was a hectic time in his life because he was stopping at the work site every day on his way to work and on his way home from work. In addition, he received around six calls a day from his contractor asking for guidance. He explains, "It was a long few months." Frank says overseeing renovations was like a part-time job on top of his full-time work.

Estimate Your Profit

Following his father into his trade, Frank went to barber school after high school. After graduation, he took a job in a women's hair salon. After eighteen months in the primarily female environment, Frank says he was ready for a change. In 1986, at twenty-one years old, he quit his job and started working in his father's barbershop. He says the experience at the hair salon was valuable. "It was good working for somebody else. It was good for seeing how good things were working for my dad."

Frank says he also prefers the atmosphere of the barbershop to the hair salon, and the pay is better, too. "If you're a good barber, and you're a busy barber, you're going to make as much if not more than what a good hairstylist is making." By working in different job environments using the skills he had learned at school, Frank was able to learn valuable specifics about the financial aspects of each business type. This experience and data allowed him to make more informed choices about the type of job and workspace he wanted to pursue for himself in the future.

MICHAEL HOLODICK, 64—FORMER BARBERSHOP OWNER

Frank's father, Michael, has always liked working in a barbershop. But prior to becoming a barber, Michael was a minor-league baseball player for five years. Once he was no longer playing ball, he was ready to earn a living outside of sports and went to work for a local shipping company, where he stayed for several years.

In the early 1970s, Michael quit his job and started his own business. Seeking better working conditions and more independence, Michael took classes to become a barber. He started his apprenticeship on Saturdays after working all week at the shipping company:

I was working at Sun Ship in Chester [Pennsylvania]. I was working in what they call the "berthing" department. It was to help speed production. We went around identifying the boats with numbers and letters, and all the crafts worked from there. It was pretty interesting.

After several years of working in the shipyards, he decided he didn't want to work outside for the rest of his life. "I knew I didn't want to be down there when I was in my fifties, or forties for that work. I thought, I'm going to need a craft; I've got to get a skill."

Make the Most of Opportunities

Michael's road to independence began when he took classes to learn how to cut hair. First, he went to barber school during the day and worked nights at the shipyard. If he went to school full time, he could have graduated in nine months, but it took him twice that amount of time to complete the program because he was holding down a full-time job and only taking classes part time. Once he finished school and an apprenticeship with a local barber, he gave his two weeks notice at the shipping company.

For four years, Holodick worked at the same barbershop where he had served his apprenticeship. When Richard's Barbershop, located one hundred feet away, went on the market after thirty years in business, Michael jumped at the chance to own his own business. "I took it over, but it took a few years to build it back up again. But we did, and everything turned out fine. And then Frank worked with me, and it was great." For the next thirty-two years, Michael made a comfortable living from his business.

For most of those years, times were good for barbers in that corner of Wilmington. Michael says there was no resentment from his former employer about setting up shop next door because there were enough customers to go around. The two barbershops thrived next door to each other for decades.

When landlord problems eventually forced the other barbershop to close, Michael says he offered jobs to the displaced barbers. "They were happy to come over with us," he explains.

Be Patient; Have Enough Capital

Michael says, in the beginning, the key to starting a new business is patience. Plus, he says a new business owner needs enough working capital to stay in business for one year. He says, "I guess that's the most important thing is to have enough capital, because you're not going to have the income every week or every month for a while." This strategy helped him to turn his business from a struggling startup into a long-term success.

His son Frank says that over the four years he has been in business, he has watched many new startups in his neighborhood quickly come and go, some in less than one year. He attributes their demise to being unprepared for the hard work a new business entails. "People just think they are going to open the door and customers are going to flock in. That doesn't happen." He says he feels lucky to have been able to keep the customers from his father's established business.

The Best Decision

Michael says that quitting his job at the shipyard and starting his own barbershop was probably the best decision he ever made. "The opportunity was there. I knew the location was good there, a lot of traffic." But opening a business was not easy:

> I was discouraged when I went in the first few months. I had a pretty good income at the shipyard. And all of a sudden, now I'm making peanuts and trying to make the overhead so my wife wouldn't have to work. She went out to work. She's a seamstress, and she went to work with this bridal shop, but I don't think she was there more than seven months or eight months. Each quarter picked up.

Once he began making enough money, Michael told his wife she could quit her job so she could stay home and take care of their young children. He says his first few months in business were slow, which made the early days of his venture a little scary. "I kept thinking, 'Oh man, I'm going to have to go back to the shipyard if this keeps up.' But every month it seemed to pick up a little bit." After one year in which his customer base steadily increased, he knew that he had made a wise decision.

Hire Good People

Along with his growing customer base, Michael credits his employees for his success. "I was fortunate to have good people working with me, the barbers." He says he couldn't have survived as a small business owner for thirty-two years without great employees."

Michael advises business owners to be flexible when they hire employees. He explains that expectations are rarely met, but good people are out there. "You never get the whole nine yards, as the expression goes. Everybody has their idiosyncrasies, their problems, their personalities, but I think that's with every craft."

Open Up to Serendipity

Michael did not always dream of being a barber. Although he realized early on that he was probably not tall enough to get drafted into the major leagues, he says his focus growing up was to become a baseball player. Through a momentary chance of serendipity, Michael's baseball path led him to cutting hair. "I went to college for just a very short time. In fact, it was so short that they gave me my tuition money back. I went to go play ball." One day, while he was in his first semester of school, he received a phone call from a minor-league baseball talent scout in Florida.

"I went down and they signed me, and it was great," Michael recalls. "Things worked out great." Suddenly, despite his average height, Michael was part of the Detroit Tigers' farm system. "I was lucky to get signed because not too many guys my size get signed. I gave them five years, and the last year I was in the Florida state link."

Michael found his future career one day while he was in Florida:

> We were playing Miami that night, and during the day I'm walking through the town. I look and I see two young guys cutting hair. This was 1965, when long hair was just starting to come in. And I thought, "Hmmm, not a bad way to make a living." I knew that was going to be my last year in ball, and I couldn't go back to college, and I thought, I'll get a trade, either like my brother the electrician, or a carpenter. So when I came [to Delaware] and got down to the shipyard, I thought, "I remember those guys in Florida cutting hair. Maybe I'll go to barber school." So that's how it happened.

Before that serendipitous moment in Florida when he saw two men making a decent living as barbers, he says he had never thought about cutting hair for a living. Even after he was taking classes in barber school, he questioned his decision. He says he wondered whether he should be taking classes to become an electrician instead. However, the business grew on him. "The more I did it, the more I cut hair, I enjoyed it. I really liked it. And the instructor was great." He said his instructor seemed to really understand where he was in his career, and taught him the value of a universal trade. Michael says the sense of autonomy that comes with being a barber greatly appealed to him, so he stuck it out and completed his training to get his license.

When Frank graduated from high school, Michael encouraged him to go to college to pursue a different career. After six months pursuing a degree in communications, Frank decided he wanted something else. His father reminded him that cutting hair is a valuable trade. So he tried it, and he liked it. That's when he enrolled in a local trade school.

After Frank finished barber school, Michael offered him a job, but Frank turned him down. Within two years, however, Frank reconsidered his father's offer and joined Michael in his barbershop. Frank enjoyed the pay raise, the lower stress levels, and fewer chemicals in his working environment.

Work Hard

Frank sees his father's situation as the classic family business: a day-by-day operation that paid for his parent's home and put his brother and sister through college. Unlike his father's initial business, Frank had the advantage of learning from his father's successes and mistakes. For example, Frank has a written business and retirement plan. He says he has tried to improve on his father's business strategy by planning more for the future. "He's sixty-six years old and still working full time. How he did it was just nose to the grindstone."

Frank says he looks up to his father for his work ethic:

To be in this business and to be successful, the people who are successful are the people like him. You have to be here. You're never sick. You take few vacations. You have to be here. That's the key to success in this business. I've seen busy barbers; they have a huge following, because it's their personality. They're reliable. They're always here. You can make a good living at it.

He adds that it is not easy to find employees who exhibit the qualities he shares with his father. He has learned that a successful barber shows up every day on time. He explains, "In twenty-five years I haven't missed three days." A strong work ethic and a quality product are two keys elements in making a business succeed.

Frank also recognizes that there are other examples of a solid work ethic in the neighborhood. Pointing across the street to Donna Rego's restaurant, the Bellefonte Café, Frank praises his neighbor's tenacity:

She's made it successful. She works her butt off. And that's the hardest thing about having your own business: It's just a lot of hours. It's the hours that I put in here cutting hair, all the bookwork, and everything else. It's cutting the grass. It's painting the railings. It's mopping the floors every week. It's all that kind of stuff. In a business like this, there's not enough [money] that I can hire other people to do it. I could, but I'm going to do it as long as I can.

To stay profitable, many entrepreneurs perform their own maintenance and housekeeping. They are never too proud to get dirty for their businesses.

Although he rarely takes a sick day, Frank does take time to enjoy a vacation every year. Because his father is a trusted employee, Frank can take ten days to go to Italy with his wife knowing his father will watch over his shop. Having his father involved in his business gives Frank the security he needs to leave his business once a year. A trusted employee offers a business owner a valuable competitive advantage since vacations are vital to a satisfying self-employment experience.

Frank enjoys working with his dad. "The thing that has made it work is we both work hard. We both have the same work ethic." He says they have both earned each other's respect by showing up to work on time for twenty years.

Frank's father also benefits from working in his son's business because it takes away the stress of running his own. Frank points out that his father no longer has to worry about things like rent and overhead. He adds, "Now he just comes in and makes his money."

Another family member who helps Frank's business succeed is his wife, Theresa, a deputy attorney general. Frank says he handles the day-to-day operations of the business because his wife is busy pursuing a career of her own. However, when it comes to any major business decisions, Theresa is always involved.

Follow the Rules

To ensure that his paperwork is filed correctly, Frank says he employs a certified public accountant (CPA) to help him do the books. A few thousand dollars every year pays for the security and peace of mind that comes with employing a professional in an area of weakness. Frank says, "It's worth every single penny." With a new understanding of the computer software QuickBooks, Frank works with his CPA every month, every quarter, and every year. He explains, "I want no worries with that." Frank says he strictly follows every rule to be a legitimate business. He says he explains this up front to every person he hires, "You get W2s, and you're going to get a paycheck. You're going to get taxed on your tips."

Sometimes following the rules makes it harder to find barbers, Frank explains, because many barbers prefer to get paid "under the table." He says he tells applicants who want to work for cash, "You go out there and you work for these other people, and see what wing nuts they are." Frank says by following the rules he offers his employees more long-term security. "You come and work for me, and you know I'm going to be here in five years."

Although he has never seen a regulatory official inside his barbershop, Frank says he complies with every state and federal law by keeping his licenses up to date and requiring all of his barbers to be fully licensed. "I don't want to lose sleep at night," he says. "That was something from the start. We're going to do it right."

Own Your Property

Owning the building where he works also gives Frank advantages his father never had. He says his father sometimes had to tolerate irresponsible barbers because he needed their business to cover the rent. Although Frank has many of the same types of headaches his father faced thanks to an unforgiving monthly mortgage payment, Frank focuses on the long-term benefits of owning the building where he does business. He says he knows his hard work today will pay off when he reaches his sixties. He says, "Not right now, but eventually, I want to be in a position where I don't have to put up with any crap."

Frank saw what his father had to put up with as a renter, so he decided to make property ownership part of his own business plan. He says owning the building gives him a great advantage over business owners who rent. The equity he builds in his business and property give him a financial edge over barbershop owners who are faced with a monthly rent bill that creates no valuable equity.

Target Your Customer

To spread the word about his business, Frank has advertised in a variety of media, including magazines, newspapers, and even on a billboard. Although he questions the value of many media outlets, one place he always advertises is in the program guides for student events at local schools. Whenever a student knocks on his door looking for sponsors, Frank says he always buys an ad. "They're a good resource. Advertising for this type of business is tough because you really need something that pinpoints just this area." He explains that he feels like he is wasting his money when he pays the high costs of advertising in local newspapers and magazines with circulations far beyond his potential customers. He points out that his target audience is only in the immediate vicinity of his shop, so advertising to a larger area is wasteful.

Frank also uses another effective advertising tool that works great for his type of small business: For more than thirty years, he and his father have sponsored a local little league team, which has generated many customers and much feedback:

> That has been great advertising. The kids come in, "I play for your team!" or "I played against your team!" When you look at the dollars, what it costs to advertise, the baseball team, now it's like $300 a year. It was $125 for years and years and years, but even at $300 it's still a great deal. You've got fifteen kids running around with your T-shirt on. They have

all kinds of programs with their schedules that have your name on it. You can't get better advertising for $300, for a small business. That's one thing I would tell any small business. That is your best $300 spent.

Keeping your money in the community also builds positive local relationships that can provide crucial support for a new business. He admits that the billboard he bought for many months was not nearly as effective and probably was not worth the expense.

Frank also uses other media to promote his business. He advertised on the radio during the Phillies playoffs by purchasing a package deal during a special promotion. He says it is hard to tell whether the $900 he spent brought in any new customers, but he still believes radio ads can plant long-term seeds in customers' minds for the future. He explains, "It might be six months from now that I get them. That's the way I look at it."

Last month, Frank launched a Web site for his barbershop with the help of his sister-in-law who specializes in computers. After planning to create a site for four years, he says he finally did it when customers told him his old phone number was coming up on Google when they searched for him. He says he is glad to finally have his Web site running, and he is still deciding whether he wants to do any additional advertising online.

Research Your Business Plan

Frank's advice to new entrepreneurs is, "Do a lot of research. Talk. Whatever business you're thinking about starting, don't be afraid to go to other people in that business and get advice. Read books." He also says that hiring a great CPA helped him get his business off the ground.

When Frank went to the bank for a loan to open his own business, he was told he needed a written business plan to get a business loan. This three-page plan needed to describe how Frank planned to earn money with his barbershop. Frank had no idea what a business plan was, so he sought the help of a CPA who could help him with his books and who promised to hold his hand through the entire process of getting his business in order. The CPA set up an S Corporation for Frank, showed him how to do payroll, and how to navigate through QuickBooks well enough to satisfy any auditor.

To help him pay his barbers, Frank says his CPA set up a system that only requires him to enter a few numbers and press the print button. "He was the only one who would do that for me."

Frank's CPA also helped him write the business plan he needed to get the small business loan. The plan included dollar numbers for anticipated earnings, revenue from the previous barbershop, anticipated expenses, and expected profits. "It was enough for the bank," Frank says. "They bought it."

The business plan for the bank also helped Frank solidify his ideas about his business:

> It helped me see what the expenses were, how much more expensive it is than I thought it would be. That never ceases to amaze me, how you just start to build money up in the bank account, and it's just one thing after another, after another. When people ask you, "Well, what kind of expenses? What is it?" It's worker's comp insurance. It's insurance on the building. It's all your licenses. It's your water bill. It's your electric bill. It's all the monthly things. But then, there are always other things. It's just one thing after another. It is more expensive than you would ever believe.

Cost overruns are common for renovation jobs and other startup necessities, so be ready for the final bill whenever working with contractors. Frank says the renovations he made to his 1914-era building cost him forty percent more than he was originally quoted.

Be There

Frank says one advantage he has over his competitors is his family's reputation for consistency. It has attracted many long-term customers over the years, to the newer location as well as the old one. He says, "They know we're going to be here."

Although Frank says his father's shop was unbelievably lucky with its employees for many years, times began to change a few years before it closed. Suddenly, many of the older barbers who had worked for him for twenty years began to retire. New barbers were only staying for six months. Some of them didn't show up. Frank says his father rarely worried about employees showing up for the first twenty years of his business. He adds, "It's not like that nowadays.

Find Your Niche

In a marketplace brimming with barber chains where high employee turnover is common, Frank says his barbershop competes by offering a place where customers can expect a barber to stick around for several years. That's the niche he's hoping to fill with his business. "There are very few barbershops like this: the old-time barbershop where it's a family business. It's going to be the same people here." He says he wants to have a barbershop where people know each other's names. He adds, "If you come in a couple of times, we're going to know who you are."

More than keeping his father's business alive, Frank says he had a vision for his own barbershop. From the very beginning, he wanted to make it a comfortable place where people can sit down and relax, like a lounge where they can get together to "shoot the breeze." He wanted to create a place with leather chairs, dark wood, snacks, and wine. He says, "I wanted a place like I would want to come to."

Learn From Your Mistakes

One mistake Frank admits he made along the way to creating a successful business was underestimating the cost of his building renovations, which went nearly $20,000 over budget. Cost overruns can be devastating to a new company, so eternal vigilance is key. This is another place positive connections can come in handy. Friends offer friends better terms. Because Frank had a close relationship with the people who did the renovations, he was able to create a flexible payment plan that allowed him to absorb the cost more easily over a longer period of time. By working with people who are close to him to create better payment terms, he gained a valuable financial benefit that helped him make his dream of self-employment come true.

Frank also credits his success to taking his time to let his business happen at its own pace, a trait that is part of his personality. Although he says it drives his wife crazy, he often takes his time to plan his next move before rushing into a big decision: "It's not that I'm not going to do it. I'm going to do it, but I'll take my time and really think things out."

Top Takeaways

1. Find a mentor. Learn from other people in the industry by tapping their expertise for lessons, skills, tools, tips, and techniques.

2. Closely consider owning versus leasing. Long leases can be a burden on a business owner, but provide an alternative to the deep commitment of a property purchase. Ownership offers equity, but can be risky in a shifting market. Consider positives and negatives.

3. Pay attention to your startup costs. More than likely, initial costs will be higher than you anticipate. Make sure you have breathing room to operate. Work hard to stay liquid.

4. Develop a vision. Know what you like and create it in your own business.

5. Make time for complications. Manage your time to include all of the extra surprises a new business will throw your way.

6. Estimate your profit. Write down your plans for your new business. Include every cost and income. Follow your money closely by budgeting and reviewing finances.

7. Make the most of opportunities. Classes or school can give you the skills you need to become more independent. Don't let a good choice slip through your fingers.

8. Be patient. Wait long enough to get the capital you need to run your business correctly.

9. Make smart decisions. Recognize an opportunity when it's staring you in the face. Seize the day!

10. Hire good people. Use your best judgment about people. You'll be depending on them for your survival. Meet them a few times before hiring them. Choose carefully.

11. Open up to serendipity. When you see something that interests you, look into it. Important things can spring from tiny moments of wonder.

12. Work hard. Every successful business owner knows that hard work is the most essential element of a solid business plan.

13. Hire a CPA. Professionals can make our lives much easier. Get referrals and ask many questions before picking the right person.

14. Target your customer. Get to know your customers by caring about them. Understand their needs and behaviors so you can create value for them.

15. Research your business plan. Read everything you can. Do some reconnaissance by shopping the competition. Talk to people who have insider knowledge.

16. Write a business plan. Write down everything you want to do. Carefully describe where you stand financially. Financial ignorance is not bliss. Write a realistic budget.

17. Be there. Show up on time and meet all of your commitments every day.

18. Find your niche. Know what you like and what you need to be comfortable. Find out from others what they like, too. Plan how your vision can work, then make it happen.

19. Learn from your mistakes. Good relationships can offer more financial flexibility.

Chapter 4

When Is the Timing Right?

hub n. *a central place where people come together*

Two doors down from the sounds of scissors snipping and razors buzzing inside the Holodicks' barbershop, music can be heard emanating from a uniquely cozy café huddled in a colorful house beneath a gnarled old tree. Patrons sit inside or on its wraparound porch while they eat, drink, smoke, play games, talk, and listen to CDs or live music on weekends. The Bellefonte Café is a comfortable local restaurant, entertainment center, and art gallery that has turned a quiet side of the street into a bustling hub of friendly faces and creative activity. It also serves some of the best food in town, if you have a few extra minutes to wait while Donna Rego, the woman who started the café seven ago, makes your guacamole fresh and stops by your table to suggest some of her famous bean soup. Her business has become a home away from home for many of her customers.

Donna's story highlights the career path of many entrepreneurs—many zigs and zags until the corporate rat race becomes so overwhelming that starting a dream business becomes a far better option.

DONNA REGO, 49—RESTAURANT OWNER

For most of her life, Donna lived in New Jersey, across the Hudson River from Manhattan. As a young adult, she decided that she wanted to move to California. Motivating her exodus from her East Coast roots was the Three Mile Island scare; the news was splashed with headlines about a possible radioactive meltdown at a nearby nuclear power reactor. Donna felt it was just the impetus she needed to leave town. Seeing the near disaster as a sign that it was time to seek out a healthier environment, Donna and her husband at the time headed to California.

With some savings in hand, they drove across the United States for more than one month. By the time they hit San Francisco, they had run out of money, so Donna became a street musician.

San Francisco was a great fit for Donna. She and her then husband decided it was where they wanted to stay, and so it was for the next ten years. She says:

> In San Francisco, after I broke up with the ex-husband and all that, I had to figure it out. So I waited tables for a while. Fisherman's Wharf is very seasonal, so after a few years of waiting tables there, they finally laid me off because wintertime was slow. Plus I don't think the mother of the owner liked my purple hair! She was very conservative.

Getting laid off from her waitressing job was the impetus she needed to create her first business. She had no idea what she was going to do; she was in her early 20s and knew she liked music. Her new boyfriend was also interested in music, including the new electronic and computerized music that was becoming popular in the 1980s. His interest in music and artistic thinking helped Donna form her first self-employment situation.

Explore Your Interests

Donna says her interest in music and her boyfriend's connections offered her opportunities to work for herself. While she was waiting tables, she was spending all of her extra money on records, forming an incredible collection. Her massive collection led to a job as a self-employed entertainer. With her collection and turntable and her boyfriend's turntable and mixer, she became a disc jockey at many local parties. She remembers, "I only did one wedding, because it was Debora Iyall from Romeo Void, so it was a big deal at the Art Institute in San Francisco. It was a cool wedding. It wasn't like a 'wedding' wedding. That was really cool."

Donna was making a name for herself as a roving DJ and printed up business cards. Soon she landed even bigger jobs in nightclubs. She liked working in the clubs because she didn't have to carry as much equipment as she hauled for her jobs at parties. "I just had to lug some records, and that was heavy."

Donna's job as a freelance DJ led to other work in the music business, including a part-time job with a record promoter and a part-time job with the "record pool," a network of DJs and promoters who paid a small fee to receive promotional copies of the latest records to play at city nightclubs. Both of these jobs helped to solidify her experience as a record industry insider.

Gain Experience in an Industry

Donna's interests, experiences, relationships, and contacts continued to propel her career in the entertainment industry. Her gigs playing dance music at clubs and her knowledge of the genre landed her a job with a record store as a buyer of 12-inch records for DJs. This connection helped her meet more people deeper inside the industry. She decided to put the word out among them that she was looking for a full-time job in the business. It was through these connections that she ended up moving to Los Angeles. Looking back, she says, "I had a lot more fun as a DJ than I did working for [the corporation]." But she had already been a DJ for eight years, so she was ready for a big change, and ready to take a chance on an exciting career move to Los Angeles. She says that she doesn't regret her decision at all: "It was cool at the time. I wouldn't go back and change a thing."

After putting the word out that she was looking for a job in the record industry, Donna received a call from an executive at one of the world's biggest record labels.

It was bizarre. They flew me down for an interview. The woman who interviewed me—I didn't even get to leave the airport in L.A.—interviewed me in that restaurant in the airport that spins around. She interviewed me and flies me back the same day. I never left the airport. So, after dinner, I flew back. And two days later she called me, "You got the job."

Donna says it was hard to leave the work and friends she had spent ten years establishing, but she wanted to see where she could take her burgeoning career.

Although she says leaving San Francisco—a city she still loves—was bittersweet, she believes it was a move in the right direction for her. "I had to do it, of course." She says that friends in Los Angeles helped her make the transition. "I moved down there and I changed my whole life."

Be Open to Opportunities

For the next eight years, Donna worked for the record label until the day she quit to start her own business. She says working for the major record label was great, at first. During the first two years she was in Los Angeles, she was working in club promotion, which was an area in which she was very comfortable thanks to her many years of experience. She was talking to DJs from across the United States, and knew their lingo. She says, "I knew what they were doing because I lived it."

Although her job was a perfect combination of her personal talents, experiences, and interests, she was quickly becoming unhappy at work as a result of conflicts with her immediate supervisor.

Donna talked to the senior vice president of promotion, who was above her boss and with whom she had a solid relationship. He wanted her to move up from club promotion to radio promotion, and said he had big plans for Donna. She recalls, "He said, 'We have an opening in the Philadelphia-Baltimore-Washington, DC, area. You'd have to relocate.'"

Make Good Moves

At this point in her life, Donna thought a move back across the country would be a great opportunity to be closer to her family and friends on the East Coast. She was already maintaining a long-distance, 3,000-mile relationship with a boyfriend in New York, so she accepted the offer. Although she was ready for a change, she admits "it was a little scary."

The job at the company's East Coast headquarters ended up being a difficult one. Once again, because of conflicts with her supervisor, she was unhappy, however the job provided her an excellent education in media. Although the job was difficult, she was excited to meet many important people in the entertainment industry. And so, despite the fact that her job was becoming more difficult by the day, she stuck with it for nearly six more years.

Start with an Exit Strategy

During her last four years in her corporate job, Donna was slowly devising an exit strategy: "I was buying all those books [like] *How to Start Your Own Business*. I was making pretty good money, and I was living up to a certain level, but I was like, 'I don't know what I am going to do after this.'"

One obvious sign of Donna's unhappiness was her state of health. To get her life back on a more satisfying track, she sought help:

> I was getting sick all the time from stress—stress-related illnesses—so I finally went to therapy. I got this social worker for the last year that I was there. I went and talked to this therapist for probably six or eight months, and just told her everything. "I don't know what to do. I've got to get out of this job. I'm really depressed. I'm sick all the time. I'm drinking too much. I'm not happy." She helped me out a lot. She totally put me on the path. I had the confidence, but she really just gave me that extra [push].

Donna says the stress from her job would keep her up at night. She began to have nightmares from anxiety in which she had lost everything she had. She was ready for a change and the first change she made was a new location.

When Donna's job moved her to the company's offices near Philadelphia, she first moved downtown. After a year in the city, she decided she wanted to live somewhere else, so she went looking for a house in a better location. Although she worked out of her house most days, she still needed to stay close to the office she used in Bridgeport, New Jersey. Someone in her office who lived in Delaware told Donna to check it out, and pointed her in the direction of Old New Castle, one of Delaware's most historic neighborhoods. Once she visited the area, she decided that she really liked it. For the next two months she drove back every weekend until she found a place to live. She rented a beautiful Brownstone building a block from the Christina River, and lived there for four years while working across the Delaware Memorial Bridge in New Jersey. She says, "My boss wasn't too crazy about it, but I was a half hour from the city. They got over it."

Donna found the place where she wanted to live and put down some roots. She says she was so stressed by her job that anything that was away from the city was perfect. Her next step was to find a way to create a job she loved. She says, "While I still had the job, I starting to try to save some money so I could buy a house in Delaware somewhere."

Do Something with It

Her Realtor took her to see a house in a small suburban town called Bellefonte, located on the outskirts of northern Wilmington. Until then, she had envisioned herself living in a more remote setting, but the idea of starting her own business helped her reconsider:

> Even though I wanted to escape and live somewhere in the woods so that I could chill out, as we were driving around looking at places, I saw a "For Sale" sign in front of this house. I said, "Pat, what about that place?"
>
> She said, "I thought you wanted remote."
>
> I said, "Yeah, but it looks like it's zoned commercial. Maybe I could do something with it."

In July 1995, Donna bought the house. By the end of the year, she was ready to quit her job:

> I told my bosses. I said, "I've got to get out of here. I'm way stressed out." They put me on a train. My boss flew in from L.A., met me in New York. My other boss met with me. They tried to talk me out of it. I said, "I can't."

They said, "A lower stress job would be way less money, and you'd have to move to New York."

I said, "Whatever. No. I just want out of here. That's it."

Donna wanted a better way to leave her job than simply quitting. Since a severance package was not going to happen, her bosses went through the process of formally firing her. "They didn't want to, but they did it for me." Collecting unemployment helped her get her feet on the ground during her first few months in business.

Because her unemployment check was just slightly more than her mortgage payment, she paid the rent while her boyfriend paid for food and expenses. Over the next five months, Donna converted the downstairs of her home on Brandywine Boulevard into an antiques store. When it was ready in May 1996, The Brandywine Trading Company became one of several resale shops on the block. For the next six-and-a-half years, she grew her company. Although she was new to the antiques industry, she read everything she could about it and learned as she went along. Her business attracted many regular customers who continue to support her. She says her company grew from a need to make a change in her life. "I figured the resale shop would be an easy place to start." What she was dreaming about now was starting her own restaurant, but she still wasn't ready. She says, "I was just scared."

Donna's vision of the perfect business became a place that served good food, drinks, music, conversation, and art. "I kind of wanted some little café. I didn't even think that I could do a restaurant." She thought she would start with pastries and coffee, and eventually grow into a full-size restaurant, but she wasn't ready to jump into a larger risk.

She says she enjoyed antiquing at the time, but it wasn't her primary goal. She had fun going to all of the flea markets, estate sales, auctions, and house clean-outs, and says she still misses doing many of those things. But she pushed her real goal to the front of her plan and realized she didn't have time for both businesses. That's when she started to focus on her top goal: starting a restaurant.

Prepare Customers for Changes

To make the transition from resale shop to restaurant, Donna started small. First she held a monthlong sale that ended with three days of complete liquidation. Donna told all of her customers what she had planned. Many remained loyal and returned after the transformation of her business.

Next, she closed her doors. Then she painted the house's interior in festive colors and designs. She enlisted a trusted friend to help her fill out the forms to get the loan she needed to upgrade her kitchen so she could create the business of her dreams.

Donna also had regulators to appease before she could get her venture off the ground. She says that worked out fine: "The board of health was relatively easy to deal with. The liquor license was harder, but it all kind of fell together once I got that loan."

Support Your Community

Decorated with art from local artists, photographers, and craftspeople, and featuring an expert mix of classic and local music—sometimes performed live by local musicians and bands—Donna's dream of creating a place where people can get together to enjoy a casual meal with good entertainment came true in 2001. She named it the Bellefonte Café.

In 2008, while reporting on the Bellefonte Café's monthly poetry night, the regional newspaper *Brandywine Community News* referred to Donna's business as "the town's epicenter of artistic expression."

Get Health Insurance

Protecting yourself from the high costs of health care or injury is part of the costs of running your own business. If you are a sole proprietor, you should keep yourself safe by carrying health insurance with a premium and co-pay you can afford. In the United States, there is generally no government program to help you pay for your hospital visits and health care needs unless you are a child, so you will need to work with an insurance company to buy the coverage you need. A number of online sites can help you compare plans and prices. Visiting sites such as geico.com, allstate.com, metlife.com, farmers.com, aaa.com, and any other insurance carrier can help you get started. Shop around. Make sure you compare your prices and coverage. If you are a freelancer, a nonprofit called Freelancers Union (freelancersunion.org) can help you plan ahead.

If you are married and your spouse is insured through his or her workplace, you can opt to be covered by that company's plan.

This is an easy way to avoid additional startup and regular business costs. If you have employees, group plans also offer discounts. Do your homework before settling on a plan, but don't put off this decision for too long. Emergencies are by nature unexpected. Don't get stuck with a devastating bill after a sudden injury. It could foil all of your dreams of self-employment.

One very risky option is to go without health insurance. Like millions of other individuals and small business owners in the United States, Donna no longer has health insurance coverage. Although she paid for health insurance coverage for many years after starting her business, one day her premiums got too high. Despite her goal of buying health insurance in the near future, Donna currently goes without health care coverage. Her situation is not unusual. She is actually just like forty-seven million other U.S. residents, or sixteen percent of the population. "I could afford health insurance for the first few years." After that, she says the cost of insurance was out of her reach.

Many small-business owners like me completely understand her dilemma. When I started my first business in California, I had no health insurance for several years. Knowing what I now know about the severe financial consequences of large health care bills, I make sure I am covered while my country remains one of the last developed nations without a universal health care system. Having a secure source of health care is a key part of remaining physically and mentally healthy. Don't save money at your body's expense. You'll need your body to keep your business alive!

Help Your People

From the moment Donna opened the doors to her restaurant until today, it has kept her extremely busy. At first she lived upstairs. When she was ready to move out of the floor above her restaurant, her first waitress moved in. By giving her waitress a really good deal on rent, she had a reliable employee nearby who worked part time. The woman's daughter and her friends also pitched in by waiting tables for tips, work experience, and fun. Donna says, "They had never waited tables before. Other friends who were also my customers before also chipped in and helped with everything." The community Donna was creating with her store and then her café helped her get her dream of a traditional restaurant off the ground.

When she was ready to expand her business to accommodate her customers with a full restaurant, they helped her do it. She says the network of friends she had been building for years kept her afloat with their support and labor while she made the changes they would later enjoy as customers and employees. Of course, Donna keeps everyone well fed with her delicious cooking as well. She says, "We're friends, and they enjoy being here."

Treating customers as friends is a strategy that has been embraced by many companies, marketing professionals, and academics. Some call it "emotional customer service" and others have referred to it as "direct marketing," but Donna's restaurant is a product of the mutual exchange of an abundance of good will. She says, "That's pretty much how it still is."

Her financial adviser is also her handyman, and her employees are her friends. They have all have made the Bellefonte Café a part of their lives. Donna says, "They all just hang out. They like being here." She says she loves the people who share her business with her every day. Donna compares the characters, camaraderie, friendships, and activities found in her restaurant to a TV comedy: "It could be better than Seinfeld! The characters are amazing. That's kind of what keeps me going."

Top Takeaways

1. **Explore your interests.** Do what you like and share it with others to find out what they think. Make connections that bring you closer to your favorite things.

2. **Gain experience in an industry.** Take your talents to new heights by focusing them on a clear career path.

3. **Be open to opportunities.** Learn everything you can from the people around you.

4. **Make good moves.** Take smart chances that could improve your career and yourself, but don't lose sight of what makes you happy.

5. **Start with an exit strategy.** Sometimes you have to make room for new possibilities by getting rid of the things that hold you back or make you unhappy.

6. Do something with it. When planning, dream of the brightest possibilities. Imagine what you could do with the opportunities that cross your path. Visualize possibilities. If they look good, make them real with solid planning.

7. Prepare customers for changes. Don't blindside people and expect them to blindly follow. Talk about your plans with your current customers. Open up to feedback.

8. Support your community. Create places and experiences you would want to be a part of even if you didn't own it.

9. Get health insurance. A catastrophic illness can be a calamity for a new startup. Protect your business by protecting yourself. Don't hold your breath for universal health care. Invest in your health. You're the only you that you get.

10. Help your people. Reaching out to your customers and employees will create loyalty like nothing else.

Chapter 5

Where Are Your Heart and Your Mind?

reputation n. **1** *one's character as viewed by the public or the community* **2** *one's good name*

Before taking the entrepreneurial plunge, you will need to "get your head straight." Putting your mind in the proper position is vital to your success. New business owners must look into their own experiences and skills to figure out where their satisfaction is found. Each of us finds our own source of career satisfaction in our own unique way. We all needed some level of self-awareness to get started in the right direction to self-employment and self-fulfillment, and it comes from a balanced combination of introspection and experience. To get there, we first searched inside our own hearts and brains to find the dreams and goals we could turn into a functional reality.

One way to do this is to get a university, college, or trade school education. Some people prefer military experience. Another way to get focused is through job experience. Basically, any well-rounded lifestyle, filled with educational and experiential opportunities taken seriously can be all that is needed to align your mind to make a small business work. Although following the rules and roles of others can help, sometimes bucking the business trends by following your own drummer can be a perfect way to differentiate yourself and your business in the marketplace. In other words, every business owner has to do what he or she thinks is best. My grandmother was right when she said, "Just do your own thing, dear."

JAMES MERVINE, 43—FAUX FINISHER/ SPECIALIST DECORATOR

My friend, known to his friends simply as Mervine, is one of those businesspeople who has always relished his independence. By following creative impulses that have taken him around the world to learn and practice his craft, he has built a successful business startup out of a well-rounded accumulation of education, connections, and experience. While following no path other than his own, he and his business have made a very successful life in London for himself, his wife, and their two children.

How does Mervine make his business successful while following his own piper? Well, he's got his "head straight" for one thing. One example of Mervine's unique success strategy is his marketing. Or, better put, his lack of marketing—an indication he knows where his strength lies, and what he wants out of a business.

Many new business owners start their companies with a flashy Web site, beautiful brochures, or even a fancy showroom. Many businesses demand these things to compete for customers. Some business owners discussed in this book, for example, rely on advertising and marketing to find customers. Others have found success with very little marketing. Some include Web sites in their marketing, others don't.

Mervine, on the other hand, does virtually no marketing.

The only marketing he has ever done for his business is to make some business cards back in the 1990s. The funny thing is that the information on the business card is incorrect. Before he hands one of the business cards to a potential client, he has to first scratch out his old information. Then he writes his new address and phone number on the back.

Because Mervine's business is based on word-of-mouth referrals and repeat customers, he says he feels that any investments in marketing would be wasted money. Every entrepreneur has to look at his or her needs before every investment to determine how much money should logically be spent to promote a business. Although some businesses require a substantial investment in sales, marketing, and advertising, others rely only on strong relationships and network connections, which are often free. Consider your options so you don't squander your cash on inefficient inroads to poor returns.

Let's look at how Mervine created a successful business while avoiding the need to spend time and money marketing.

Get Realistic

Mervine quit his job as a day laborer in the construction industry and started his own company ten years ago. He has been very successful ever since. He is so successful he seems almost embarrassed by his recent accumulation of wealth. As an expert at applying an interior wall treatment known as "polished plaster," as well as a variety of other professional paint finishes, his many customers pay very well for the lovely results of his time-consuming work. How did the son of a popular schoolteacher and a devout stay-at-home mother from rural Delaware become a successful business owner in London? He says his preparation for his current job began back at the University of Delaware where he studied art, but his first focus after college was not starting his own business. Mervine was more interested in starting a successful rock-and-roll band.

Mervine says, "I tried being a rock star in the 1980s and early 1990s with very minor success." He explains that he had a cousin who did the type of specialty plaster work that he would end up doing in his own business:

> It's called "faux finishing" in America. In England it's called "specialist decoration." Mainly it's polished plaster, but I started off getting into it with paint finishes, like antique drag, and making new things look old. Sometimes it's copying marble, like if somebody had some woodwork in their house and they want it to look like marble. I paint it to look like marble or wood, and gilding and stuff like that.

While he still lived in the United States, his cousin introduced him to the process. The skill piqued his interest. He then met a woman while he was in college who also did faux finishing. He says, "In the back of my mind, I always thought, you know, one of these days I'm going to have to get serious about getting a real job, and when I do, I'll just do that."

Mervine says, "So, time went on, and it was obvious I wasn't going to make a living as a rock star or an artist, and then I got married. Then I thought, well, time to dig in." Once Mervine received permanent residency status in England—thanks to his marriage to a UK citizen—he knew it was time to step up to the plate and start earning more money.

That's when he started to gather everything he needed to know to get started on a new career. "I got a bunch of books about decorative paint finishes and I got a bunch of pieces of board and just started doing samples, just copying the effects I saw and just phoning anybody in the phone book or any interior design magazine that I thought might be helpful."

Review Your Plan: Get Expert Advice

Next, Mervine called a few local interior designers and asked them if he could come in and show them his portfolio of sample designs. One expert in London provided Mervine with a valuable critique of his decorative painting sample boards. This feedback helped him learn more about his areas of strength and weakness.

His big break came when he showed his boards to another interior design expert. The designer said she had a job for somebody who could travel to Saudi Arabia. She told Mervine that she needed men to accompany her workers because they were all women, and every woman who goes to work in Saudi Arabia needed to be accompanied by a man.

Although he agreed to travel to Saudi Arabia, the job fell through. But the contractor called Mervine back about another job, "Then she had a job that she just needed people to work cheap and travel to Jordan to decorate the King of Jordan's palace, so I did that. That was my very first job." While working in the home of the King of Jordan, Mervine found that he got along really well with the contractor. He also learned that he has a talent for specialist decoration. When he got back to London, the designer started hiring him regularly as a self-employed artisan.

With a great reputation for hard work, Mervine kept receiving regular work and higher rates. Eventually, he started running jobs for the designer.

Build Relationships and Connections

Although he was also working an occasional job for other contractors and clients, Mervine found that the owner of a specialist decoration firm had become his best customer. He was working for her nearly full time, and sometimes more. Although she had a handful of full-time employees, she also employed many other people, like Mervine, who she would bring in on big jobs. Mervine explains, "She liked me and she saw that I was good." He had built his most important business relationship and his business was humming along nicely.

Mervine's affability, talents, and networking skills helped him keep his business growing. His primary customer was great at delegating work, and Mervine was happy to take on tasks. He liked the independence of managing a work site however he saw fit. He says, "She let me really deal with it, which was really great. She was really talented and really taught me a lot about paint finishes and things."

Eventually, Mervine's main customer got married and moved to South Africa. When she left, a man who had his own firm with whom she worked took over her business. Mervine explains that there are two types of people who do his type of work. One type is a bohemian college-educated artist type of worker who comes at the work from an artistic direction. The other type is more of a working-class type of worker who goes to a trade school to learn stippling, dragging, and gilding. Mervine says, "They work on places like Buckingham Palace and big official buildings. I guess years ago they would have been in a guild." Although Mervine fits into the first category, he says the new owner was from the latter group. Mervine could see times were changing. An event that could have been a setback for Mervine's new business suddenly became a boon.

When one of the other company's customers was unhappy with its change of management, the interior designer approached Mervine. Because the designer had worked with Mervine before, he trusted his work. The interior designer asked Mervine if he could take on his workload. Mervine recalls, "It caused a bit of a rift with some of the people I work with, but I thought, I've kind of got to go for it." He explains that he has since made up with those people, but this decision helped him get his foot securely in the door of a successful self-employment opportunity.

Once he agreed to take on the interior designer's work, Mervine stopped by the job site and priced the job. The designer accepted his offer, so he pulled together the people he needed to get the job done. "Then I started calling my self-employed friends, and they started working for me," he says. Mervine's connection with the interior designer turned into his most important business relationship, replacing the one that moved to South Africa.

Create Trust

One reason why Mervine continues to enjoy his job today is because it really suits his skills, personality, and lifestyle. He explains, "I have an art background, I'm really creative, I'm good with color and paints, so I'm good with the paint finishes." He is also still strong enough and physically capable of the hard labor involved in applying polished plaster. Plus, Mervine believes, his middle-class status helps him appeal to wealthy clients who prefer to work with artists rather than laborers. He says, "I always let it be known that my background is in art. I know how to kind of play the game now."

Mervine says that his nationality also pleases customers in a weird way. "I'm finding that being an American is a real help to me, because it's a bit exotic. People are like, 'Why is this American guy working on our job site?' but they kind of like that." Mervine says that his lack of a British accent actually works in his favor when battling the competition. He explains that a person's accent is really scrutinized in England. Because he doesn't have a working-class British accent, people are unable to pigeonhole the class status of his East Coast American accent. He says, "In England, people can place you immediately by your accent, so if you have a working-class accent, people will always think of you as a working-class person, no matter what your job or income level is. The fact that I am 'class-free' is very helpful to me."

Beyond his ambiguous class status, Mervine says there are a few more important reasons why he is successful: "I do what I say I'm going to do. I have a really good reputation. Plus, I'm really good at what I do. I've just learned that I'm in this game where people like to pay a lot of money, so I obligingly charge them a lot of money!"

Price Your Work Competitively

To determine a competitive price for his products and services, Mervine says it was easy to do the research and the math. First, he talked to some other polished plaster people, found out what they were charging, and started charging accordingly. To determine a price for his polished plaster work, he just measures the walls and charges per square meter. When pricing a paint finishing job, he simply calculates how long he thinks it will take based on his past experiences. He says, "I just think of how many days it will take to do the job and tack on a little extra for insurance. I figure out how much money I want per man-day."

As many entrepreneurs discover, figuring this out was difficult when he was just getting started, Mervine says:

> Oh God! It was a nightmare at first. I was very panicked about it. I charge a lot of money, and at first it was a bit weird for me to give these great big prices to people. Then they would just shrug and say, "Okay." Some people balk and say that it is too much, but it's fine. In my game, you kind of have to be expensive because if you're too cheap, they'll think you're too low-rent.

He explains that finding out a proper price was just a matter of picking people's brains. Talking to other people in his industry taught him many of the tricks of the trade he uses every day, including pricing bids. He says, "If you put in outrageous prices and too many people say no, then you just drop your prices."

Demonstrate Your Skills

It took Mervine about six months from the time he made the choice to quit his job as a laborer on a job site to the day he lined up his first paying gig as a self-employed professional. He explains, "Once I got legal, I specifically only took temporary work. I knew that there was a possibility that somebody would offer me two weeks' work." He says that he specifically took short-term assign-ments so he would be available for his own business if and when the time came. This allowed him to take the job in Jordan when it unexpectedly landed in his lap. He recalls: "I got my first break going to Jordan. Then it started to stay quite steady after that. I started doing polished plaster in late '98 when that guy actually asked me to come and start doing work for him, and really start getting my own crew together." It took Mervine five years from the time when he first started doing specialist painting to the time he started getting his own crews together in 2002, around the same time his daughter was born.

After eleven years of working for himself, Mervine says he feels like he has stumbled into a job that fits him perfectly. He explains, "It just happens to be a job that really suits me." Although he sees opportunities to make his business grow even larger, he doesn't want to get too big:

> To be honest with you, I'm not really that ambitious. I've never advertised. I've never tried to get work, other than when I first started. I've never had to hustle up work. Also, I have a number of designers that hire me now because, just over time, I've met people. Some people give me two really nice juicy jobs every year, some people give me one a year. Some people give me two, three, four little jobs a year. Then mainly I work for this one main guy.

Mervine explains that his success comes down to a few basic fac-tors that he works hard to maintain every day, including reliability, talent, and self-confidence: "For me, the main thing is I'm reliable. I'm just good at it. When I first got into it, I thought, I can do this. And it turns out that I really can! I'm really good at it."

Get Education and Training

When it comes to professional training, Mervine says he believes in the value of a solid liberal arts education, like the one we both received at the University of Delaware, where we both got our bach-elor's degrees in arts and science.

After graduating from high school in rural Seaford, Delaware, where his father taught science, Mervine moved north to Newark where he went to the University of Delaware. He explains that the education he received at Delaware continues to help him in his work today, and gives him a leg up on his competition. "It helps to be a university-educated person in a working-class environment. I think that's helped me," he explains. He also says that this is probably a British thing. "I don't know how it would be in America, but I think being an educated person in a realm where most people are not expected to be educated has been a real boon for me. So I'd say, 'Stay in school kids!'"

The University of Delaware was the last formal education Mervine needed to make his business a success. The only other additional formal schooling he has received since then was a day with his plaster supplier: "When I first learned polished plaster, in order for this company to sell this plaster to me, they made me come down and do a little class. I literally spent one day with them. They kind of just want to check you out."

Capitalize on Good Luck

Along with his early education and experiences living and working in a variety of jobs and cities around the globe, Mervine says there is another ingredient in his formula for success: "To tell you the truth, a good chunk of what happened to me was luck: I was lucky I met this woman to go to Jordan. Through her, I also found out about polished plaster because of working in some very high-class environments."

Mervine's good fortune also involves his ability to make positive connections and create relationships with other people. He explains:

> The way I got into polished plaster was, while working for this company, I met one of the women who worked for them. She was a secretary, but she also worked on site, and we got on quite well. She quit that company and went to work for another company in the same business, for a guy who was trying to get a crew together, and she just called me up and she said, "Hey! This guy's trying to get a crew of people together to learn to do polished plaster. Would you like to learn?"

He did. By recognizing and jumping at this opportunity, Mervine met his friend's connection, a contractor who introduced Mervine to the supplier of the ingredients and supplies to make polished plaster. This was the key connection he needed to start his own business. Although Mervine didn't get along well with the contractor and never worked with him again, he still helped Mervine immensely by introducing him to the people who sold polished plaster. For one day, Mervine trained to use their product. Today, many years later, Mervine remains one of the supplier's regular customers. He explains he took his new skills to another interior design firm and was hired to do polished plaster for the firm's clients.

After six years of working together, that interior designer remains Mervine's biggest customer.

Mervine says that luck played a big role in his good fortune, but after some reflection, he adds, "It was a lot of luck, but it was also taking my lucky breaks and really running with them." Although he is modest about his ambitions, Mervine says: "I was quite determined to do this. I just basically saw that you could make good money at it. And, you can. The last couple of years have been fantastic."

Get the Timing Right

Timing has also been an important part of his remarkable success, Mervine explains. He points out that he just happened to get his business started at the beginning of one of the most incredible economic booms in the history of mankind. As the provider of a luxury service, he has been able to create value for the wealthy customer base that has more money than ever to spend on his work. "It just happened that I started in '97, which is when things just started to pick up and go crazy. I just happened to be right there."

Although he has been more successful than he ever imagined possible, Mervine doesn't see himself as particularly ambitious. He doesn't want his company to grow too large. He has learned from experience that too many jobs can create headaches and hassles he would rather avoid:

> There have been times when I've had like three big jobs on the go at once, and you get to a certain point though, if you're not actually doing all of the work yourself, and you're subbing everything out, you don't make nearly as

much on a job. I would much rather have one big job that I was working on, there every day, and hiring the people, and sorting out. I would much rather have that than three huge jobs where I was just too busy to do any of them, and I was hiring everybody.

Set Realistic Limits

Over time, every new business owner learns to set limitations on his or her work. Sometimes those lessons come at the expense of a customer or two, which is part of the learning process. Along the way to his current success, Mervine learned that being too busy can sometimes cost him clients. Customers like a personal touch, but sometimes a business owner can't be everywhere a customer wants him or her to be. Mervine says one customer stopped calling when he was unable to spend all day at his job site because he had others going on as well: "He started using me, so we had a good rapport, but he started using me just at a time when I was really slammed with work, and I wasn't able to give the personal attention that he wanted. And he doesn't use me anymore because he wanted *me* to do it."

One limitation that Mervine sets for himself is the number of hours he wants to work each week. He says he is not willing to work eighty hours a week:

> I have done it, but I don't want to do it. I think that if I had actually decided I really want to make a go of this and see how far I can push it, I'm sure I could have gotten a real slick Web site, and a slick brochure, and gone around and really wheeled and dealed, and met designers. They have these big design shows all over London where designers go, and you meet people. I could have done all that and really made a push, and then got a crew that just worked for me, and just got the work and went around and saw that it was done right, and did the samples. That's not me. I like working with my hands. I got into it because I thought I'd be good at the work.

Although many entrepreneurs are motivated solely by money, Mervine had different goals in mind when he chose his current profession. "Don't get me wrong: I like to make decent money, but I'm not so motivated by money that I only want to do the paperwork and business side. That's not my thing. It's not what gives me satisfaction. I like doing the work. Of course, I like getting paid, too."

Develop a Great Reputation

Mervine has been getting paid to do what he loves because he satisfies his customers with high-quality work. Word of mouth saves him marketing and advertising costs. He knows that when people find good people, they stick with them. He says, "I'm very good, and I'm reliable; I think that's been my biggest calling card, really: I have a great reputation in the business."

That's the reason why, after five years at his current address, he still has not even invested in new business cards. He apparently doesn't need them. But the road to success has not been perfectly smooth for Mervine. He says, "It's not all been like me skipping down the road collecting paychecks." There was a time two years ago when he was working harder than he had ever imagined. He was swamped with so much work that he was driving between three distant job sites every day for several weeks, rarely getting home for a break. He says, "It was driving me crazy!" But his persistence paid off. He's learned that, although his business gets hectic during its busiest months, his business follows a strange type of ebb and flow, so he rides out busy or difficult weeks with hard work and patience. "It does happen occasionally, and I just have to get through it, and grin and bear it. Then it usually calms down. It always just calms down. Usually, I just have one big job and a couple of small jobs on the go here and there," he says.

Make a Plan and Run with It

Mervine attributes much of his success to luck, and the fact that he has happened upon a job at which he excels. "It just turns out that I fell into this: everything that I do, and that I'm all about, is just perfect for this job. And when the opportunities did come up, I really ran with them."

Mervine sometimes wonders what kind of business he might have created if he were more ambitious, but finds himself satisfied with the way it is working today. He's doing extremely well in a competitive field. The risks he could have taken by becoming a larger operation could have cost him his core customers who rely on his personal touch. Growth also brings more management responsibilities with employees and job sites, taking away his time doing a craft he enjoys. Plus, with a larger operation, he might also have to sacrifice the time he spends with his family, which is his top priority.

Give the People What They Want

One reason for Mervine's company's success in London might be his casual business style. He explains:

> Not making an effort is a real asset in England, and I don't think that it would be that much of an asset in America. This is only conjecture because I've never really worked there as a professional, but I think in America they're like, "I liked that guy because he was a real hustler. He was really hustling. I really liked that." But over here, it's like, "If you have to try that hard, why aren't you busy?" The rule of thumb over here is, if you call a builder and ask him to do some work on your house, if he says he can start tomorrow, don't hire him. Any good builder in London will be booked up over a year.

Mervine believes that his casual attitude toward sales and marketing has really helped him because not seeming to make an effort has worked in his favor. His customers seem to respect that he lets the quality of his work speak for itself. When potential customers ask for his Web site address, brochure, or pictures of his work, Mervine tells them he's been too busy to get these things together. He doesn't need them. He explains, "That really works over here, and I don't know how well that would work in America."

Mervine says Londoners seem to appreciate when businesspeople do their work their own way and on their own terms. He adds, "I think people really like that and respect that."

Work with Other Freelancers

Looking at the broader picture of his company's plan in his local business environment, Mervine explains that working only with other freelance professionals rather than hiring full-time employees has been another key to his success. Mervine says:

> It is just pure capitalism: It's just supply and demand. There are a lot of efficiencies to that. My business would be totally different if I had to hire four people full time. Every now and then I'll get a great big job, and I'll need five people for five weeks. When that job's over, if the next job is a little one-man job for me for two weeks, I don't need those people. Everybody knows that. I say that when this job comes to an end, "You give me your invoice; I'll pay you. See you later."

Many of the freelancers who work for Mervine also employ him as a freelancer when their own companies need additional people for a contracting job. "Some of the guys who work for me will get a big job and they'll say, 'I need some help.' I'll say, 'Here's my day rate.'"

Using subcontractors as workers is a flexible business strategy that works well for Mervine's company. Although some subcontractors can be expensive, he'll hire them when he needs the help on a polished plaster job. Sometimes he trades his own work for their work. These arrangements help him survive and thrive. He says:

> Everybody is self-employed, and it's good. If I had to keep four people busy all the time, then I would be forced to go track down business. If I had to do people's insurance and all kinds of stuff, then it would just be totally different. I would have to approach things just completely different. As it is now, I don't have to.

Note. In the United States, the IRS and Social Services Administration, as well as state and local labor departments, take a dim view of companies that hire people and call them "independent contractors" as a means to avoid paying payroll taxes, getting workers' compensation insurance, and so forth. You can get hit with back taxes and stiff penalties if you misclassify the people who work for you. Before you base a business on hiring independent contractors, get a qualified opinion as to the legality of your scheme.

Recognize Your Physical Limitations

Now that he has entered his forties, Mervine says he is beginning to think about changing his business plan to accommodate his increasing age. One issue he faces is the physical ability of his body because his work has many physically demanding aspects. "I can't do this until I'm sixty-five. Maybe paint finishes, but most of my work is polished plaster. It's a very physical job. I think I've got another maybe ten years, if that. I can't see myself much into my fifties doing this."

He says he is just beginning to develop his long-term plan for dealing with the issue of performing physically demanding work with an aging body. One idea that is just beginning to take shape is a business that makes the most of his contacts and skills in the interior design industry. Before he throws out his back doing his current job, he wants to establish a less-physically-taxing career.

As an accomplished sculptor and artist, Mervine's vision of his life as an entrepreneur extends well beyond his current work and into other creative realms. Right now he is pursuing his interest in interior lighting by researching chandeliers. "I want to start to get into making lights, something studio-based where I'm still making stuff, working with my hands, and in interiors." He adds, "I think if I can do cool, hand-made, bespoke, one-off kinds of chandeliers, as long as I can find the right person to sell it, I think I could do really well. I'd really like to, ideally, do that: get a really cool studio-based business where I'm not out on site all the time and still in interiors."

But Mervine says he's not in a big hurry to change career paths just yet: "I'd like to ease into it. What I'm going to start doing is try to start making some lamps now and see how it goes, see what they look like, see if there's any viable plan."

Lately, Mervine pursues information about his new interest while remaining watchful for suppliers of the types of materials he might need to start his new niche business. When he's not working, Mervine's involved in this type of important research and development.

Work Hard

When he is working, the true cornerstone in his successful business plan is the hard work he puts into his job every day. Some days, he says, a full day of hard labor wears him out:

> I'm beat today. When I work on my own, I don't take many breaks. And I knew I was going to have to go off to this other job today. The client was there all day, so I didn't want to seem to be sitting around sipping tea all day, and then knock off early. So, I get in, I hustle, and I take a twenty-minute lunch break. Then I skip my afternoon tea break, and then I shoot off to the other job for a couple of hours. Today, I got up at 6:30 A.M. and I just got in the car and went. I didn't really stop until I got home at 6:00 P.M. I'm exhausted now.

Although Mervine tries to keep his work out of his weekends, it doesn't always work out that way. Sometimes he has to work on a Saturday. But he's not bothered by a stray weekend of work. "I'm not that freaked out about going in on Saturday. If I was really busy, busy, busy, and then I had to go in again, I might be a bit p——off, but I had a few months this year that I didn't work." While working in the fluctuating business of interior finishing, he says he has learned to enjoy the weeks he has off because he knows how hard he will be working when the jobs begin to flow again, as they do during every upswing in their periodic cycles. Until then, he says he'll enjoy the extra time off by spending it with his wife and children.

Top Takeaways

1. Get realistic. Hone your dreams down to a realistic plan that can comfortably support you and your family. If it can't, keep your day job.

2. Review your plan: Get expert advice. Talk to people in the industry in which you want to work and show them how much value you can add to their businesses.

3. Build relationships and connections. Do the quality work that keeps customers coming back for more.

4. Create trust. Build trust in your customers by working hard and doing the things you say you are going to do.

5. Price your work competitively. Set your prices high enough to make a living, but low enough to keep your customers happy. Finding this middle ground might take a few tries to get right.

6. Demonstrate your skills. Show your clients that you can do what they need. Prove to them that they can count on you by providing quality work.

7. Get education and training. A well-rounded education is respected around the world. Exploit your expertise and accomplishments as a learner.

8. Capitalize on good luck. Jump at the opportunities that will introduce you to the people who can help you succeed. Don't slack off.

9. Get the timing right. You'll know that your timing is right because you'll find yourself faced with coordinating more work than you ever imagined. Stay on top of your schedule!

10. Set realistic limits. Never make a promise you can't keep. Be realistic with your clients about the work you can do.

11. Develop a great reputation. Referrals and repeat business can keep you afloat.

12. Make a plan and run with it. Jump at opportunities and follow through with the plans you make.

13. Give the people what they want. Feel out your industry and find a style that makes you valuable in the eyes of your customers.

14. Work with other freelancers. Building a network requires give and take. Take care of your colleagues and they will take care of you when the shoe is on the other foot.

15. Recognize your physical limitations. Don't overdo it. Keep your body safe from harm so you can enjoy the fruits of your labor. Plan to slow down one day.

Chapter 6

How to Quit Your Job

salubrious adj. *offering the benefits of good health or well-being; full of health, good, salutary, etc.*

salutary adj. *1 offering good health; full of health. **2** offering a good reason; full of benefits*

When I first met Weese Wagner, I couldn't see her face, but I could hear her strong, soothing voice from across the room. I was sitting on a mat in the back of a packed yoga class, my first, and the voice of the instructor beckoned me to relax in such mellifluous tones that I immediately felt my blood pressure drop and my muscles unwind. My wife had been raving for months about her wonderful instructor at a new yoga studio in town, so I decided to finally take her up on her request for me to join her in a "hot power yoga" class. Since then, I look forward to opportunities to take Weese's sweaty yet enjoyable class.

MARIE "WEESE" WAGNER, 48—YOGA STUDIO OWNER

Weese has been the sole proprietor of a yoga studio in Wilmington, Delaware, since opening her doors more than five years ago. When she quit her job in the corporate world to start her own business, she was carrying out a plan that was many years in the making, whether she knew it or not.

Be Practical...

Raised in a traditional, practical-minded, Catholic-Italian family, who always urged her to get a professional job in a good company with health care benefits, Weese says, "I always thought that was the route you had to go. So I went about my business."

When she got her driver's license as a teenager, Weese started teaching aerobics and other fitness classes on weekends at local gyms. Through this part-time job, she got her first exposure to other self-employed business owners. "At the time, this was in the '70s, there was a center called Living Well Lady. It's now out of business." Although she enjoyed teaching fitness classes, she never imagined herself pursuing fitness as a full-time career.

...But Think Outside the Box

After high school, Weese continued on her traditional trajectory. "I did the whole thing, went to college, got a business degree. I came from the mindset where you have to get a job at IBM or something like that." Although she worked hard to earn her general business degree in 1982 from Millersville State University in southeastern Pennsylvania, she says she was not very passionate about business. "I just thought it was something you had to do. It was the way you went," she says. She thought a business degree would keep her employed after college, so she took the practical path of least resistance. "I wasn't thinking outside the box then," she adds.

After college, Weese rose through the ranks at a variety of large corporations as an executive assistant, marketing coordinator, and other professional jobs. Finally, she found a secure job at a large global corporation. But one day, after eleven years as a loyal employee, she realized she needed to quit. Although she enjoyed the people with whom she worked, she was not enjoying the restructuring process that was becoming a continual headache at work.

Weese had continued to teach fitness classes at nights and on weekends while she worked full time in the corporate world. She found that teaching fitness and health was something she truly loved. "That's what I had fun with," she says. "Long ago, I toyed with the idea of, 'wouldn't it be nice to someday own a gym?' But I never thought of it as anything practical, so I kept my practical job."

But during one of the company's many restructuring efforts, Weese's job was phased out. She was moved to a different marketing assistant position with different responsibilities at a different location. She explains: "Then they started restructuring [again]. One day, they just came in and they were going to make a change to my job that would have made me uncomfortable."

Nurture Your Ideas with Formal Training

While considering the changes to her corporate job, Weese thought back to an idea she had five years earlier. She says:

I had actually been giving more serious thought to maybe someday opening a yoga studio, because I'd always done yoga since I was a teen. In 1992, I became more serious about yoga than any of the other things I was teaching. I just saw all the benefits of yoga versus other activities that you could not do as you aged. You become older, you can't really do aerobics. You can't go jogging. I saw how these things could actually damage the body. Yoga was completely different, and I became more submerged in yoga at this point.

Many businesses ride the wave of new, popular trends, banking on them taking hold in the wider community. In the early 1990s, yoga's popularity and predominance in the fitness industry was just beginning to spread to the East Coast. Suddenly, Weese saw a couple of yoga studios pop up in her area, sparking her increasing interest in the fitness practice.

Although she was beginning to make yoga a daily part of her life, this form of exercise still had not caught on with the general population. Weese explains, "It wasn't popular then, probably in California, but not around here. The classes I went to were small."

Weese pursued her new passion every day:

I personally submerged in the study of yoga, teacher training, doing yoga, that kind of thing. I saw the benefit that it could bring to a person, and believed in it. It's one of the few activities you can do well into your old age, and it just has so many benefits, so I was getting into it more and more and more along those levels, on a personal level.

Watch for Marketplace Changes

By 1996, Weese saw more yoga studios open up nearby, each featuring a different style of yoga. That was when she discovered "hot power yoga." More people were attending classes. Suddenly, she began to see more prospects for a business in hot power yoga. Still, she was not consciously thinking about a major career change or opening a studio. Weese says, "I had a job, and I saw these people now starting to come into these yoga classes, and I thought, boy, this would be really cool. I always said these kinds of things to my husband."

Quit Your Job When It's Time to Go

One day, things began to change at Weese's corporate job. "They told me again that they were restructuring my job, and things were just so up in the air. After a number of years of restructuring, it just really upset me," Weese recalls. "I didn't like the change they were making to my job, and I did something completely out of character for me, and I quit my job."

Before she quit, she tried to reason with her bosses:

> I basically told them, "I really don't like this change you're making. I'm not comfortable with it." It was a different reporting structure, and they were going to be making more types of task changes to the job. I really liked the people I was working with and working for, but they were changing that department, too. I didn't like the area I was going into.

A new boss entered the picture. When he started chopping heads and reshuffling employees, Weese's job became unbearable. She asked her new boss for a compromise in a new work arrangement that made her uncomfortable, but he refused her requests. "Everybody was just very unnerved. It was a very tough time at this place, and, I don't know why, I just kind of quit."

Reach Out to a Trusted Confidant

The conflict with her boss was the culmination of several difficult months at her job. Weese began to complain more often to her husband, Mark, about her dissatisfaction at work. She explains, "He saw how upset it would get me, and so on. And he just kept saying,

'Quit your job. Quit your job. You'll get something else. Quit your job.' It just kind of all accumulated all at once, and I just quit my job."

In the past, Weese says she had quit jobs to take other positions that were already lined up. This time, she simply called an end to a bad employment relationship without worrying about her future employment. "I can't even believe I did it, to this day, because it is just so out of character for me," she adds.

Along with enough experience, skills, and will to start her own job, Weese also had a secret weapon that many small business owners have up their sleeve, which allows them to impulsively reach for their best dreams: a supportive partner. A spouse with a solid job that includes family health and other benefits can be the steady foundation on which to climb into a better work situation. This type of leverage can strengthen the backbone of confidence an entrepreneur needs to quit a job. Sometimes, a deeply committed relationship, whether marriage or otherwise, refined over years building a happy and financially stable home life together, is the vital ingredient needed to help a business owner become self-employed.

Get Support

Before I quit my last job, Michelle Lauer, my wife of ten years, also chanted the quit-your-job mantra whenever I complained about working in my cubicle. While making her emotional support clear, she also made her financial support apparent by telling me that she would be able to change her work to accommodate my new business. If we needed to switch our health care coverage from my employer to hers, the option was available. This type of support in my back pocket made my final decision to quit my job much easier and the transition to my new job much smoother.

As a gainfully employed nurse, my wife could easily move from a part-time position to a full-time one in an organization in which her career as a nursing leader has flourished. She was ready to take on the added responsibilities in an organization whose mission she shares. By shifting our family's insurance to her employer, we not only saved money for my business, but we ended up getting better health care coverage for our family.

When Weese quit her job in the corporate world, her husband Mark had a solid job that included health benefits, which gave

Weese the financial support to help her survive between her abrupt departure and her next source of income. Only a few years before, Mark had gone back to school to get his engineering degree. When Weese decided to quit her job, her husband was still in the first couple of years of his new job. Weese knew she was taking a financial risk by quitting her job and starting her own business. She says, "It was really kind of gutsy for me to quit, because this was his first job out of college that he was in for a few years. It's not that we were so set, as if we both had been working all these years, and we had all these plans, and that kind of thing: It was an awful lot to put on him."

Dream Big

On the day she quit, Weese says she still did not have a clear plan of what she would do next. She imagined that she would get another corporate job and continue to teach yoga part time. But her husband, the dreamer, intervened. She explains:

> He's very positive; he's a dreamer. He's the go-for-it type. Me, I'm always looking at reasons why you shouldn't go for it. Be safe. But he's the one. I got home and he's like, "Well, for years you have been teaching yoga, talking about how it'd be a nice business. Everything is aligned. Now's the time to do it, because, I know you, if you don't do it now, you're going to just get another job."
>
> The corporate world was never really my passion or my interest. He said, "I know you. You'll get another job and you'll just go through the days like you've been doing. Now's the time. If you want to try this, now's the time to do it."

Like a good partner, Weese's husband challenged her to step up to her own dreams. He allowed her to see possibilities that she might not have seen for herself.

Once she quit her job, she began to contemplate the reality of starting her own business. She was plagued by doubts about her possibilities for success. But her husband continued to help her overcome her fears by keeping her positive. She adds, "If it wasn't for his support, I never would have done it."

Go with the Flow

Weese's next step toward self-employment was to create a source of spending money. She took a part-time job taking care of plants for an interior design company. Weese says this job gave her a comfortable zone between career moves where she could realistically consider her options. Meanwhile, she was looking around town for a possible location for her future yoga studio. She explains that yoga helped her get through this stressful part of her self-employment adventure. Through yoga, she learned to remain calm and to try to go with the flow. "Yoga teaches you all these things. I was really trying to live my yoga and just see where this river took me."

Although Weese was looking for a place to start a yoga studio and had a part-time job, she hedged her bets by sending her résumé back into corporate America. She even interviewed at a few large companies. During the interviews, she realized that she really didn't want to spend her days sitting in another cubicle in the corporate world.

She said her husband's positive encouragement reverberated in her mind. "I just kept hearing Mark's words in my head. 'This is the time to make this change that you've always been casually mentioning. This is the time or you're never going to do it.'"

Tap Your Resources

Weese spent the next few months looking at a variety of possible studio spaces in several nearby towns, but their rent was much too high. She wasn't willing to take on the added risk of a high rent bill. One day, she stumbled on a possible space that could become a comfortable little yoga studio. The place needed much work to make it functional, but the rent was reasonable. Weese recalls, "It was pretty much a dump."

Luckily, she had somebody who could help: her husband, Mark, the construction engineer. He volunteered to help her clean up the place, make improvements, and get her business off the ground with whatever services and skills he could offer. Although Weese feared the prospect of a long, costly lease, as well as the giant task of turning a neglected storefront into a working yoga studio, her husband's offer to assist helped her get closer to her dream job.

Better yet, it had something besides a reasonable rent to make it attractive: room to expand if everything went well.

Limit Your Risk

So Weese jumped into self-employment by signing a one-year lease. She didn't want to take on the risk of agreeing to anything longer than one year. Next, she took her husband up on his offer to help her build a yoga studio. "He was cursing the place out as we actually got into it." Once hardwood floors, a heating system, ceiling fans, benches, and other infrastructure were installed, Weese hosted her first hot power yoga classes.

Starting with limited classes, she kept her part-time job taking care of plants while she built up her clientele. Her paycheck from her part-time job could cover the studio's rent, which helped her overcome her fear of the new monthly rent bill. She had committed to a year as a business owner. She called her new company Yoga U.

Weese says that her business worked out better than she expected. "I love teaching yoga classes. Whenever I was there teaching, I was just happiest and the most comfortable."

At first, she worried whether people would attend her classes. She knew that when she taught classes in other places, she was working with a captive audience. There had always been an established clientele at the gym or yoga studio. Suddenly, it was up to Weese to attract and retain a group of customers who could help support her business. She says this was a new challenge for her. She explains, "It's very different getting people who don't know you to walk in the door."

Adjust to Customers' Needs

Weese says she understood many of the hurdles and challenges she faced:

> You have to make these people want to get in their car and drive to your class. It's a completely different mind-set you have to develop, versus, say, teaching in a gym or teaching at a studio where they already have people walking in the door. I was petrified of that.

Once again, her chosen profession helped her succeed. "I just tried, again, to live my yoga and to keep in mind how much I believe in yoga, and how much I enjoy teaching yoga classes," Weese says. Her strategy worked at both keeping her happy and attracting the clientele she needed to survive. An increasing number of people turned up to join her classes. Some never returned, but others began to return again and again.

By listening to her clients and applying their feedback to her classes, Weese was beginning to get the hang of her new business. Meanwhile, she adapted to her customers' needs:

> I would adjust, because you have to adjust to who's walking in your door. I was actually thrilled, because many of the other places I had taught, a lot of them had very young clientele. I was in my forties at this point. I was used to a very young clientele, but when I opened my doors, what I saw were people walking in the door who were in their forties. I was actually thrilled at that, because that was more *me*. That was more how I wanted to teach yoga.

Weese explains that different age groups have different needs. Twenty-year-olds want a vigorous workout. More mature people want a tough class, too, but Weese says she has found that they want other benefits from her yoga classes beyond a strenuous butt-kicking. "You have people who might have a back that bothers them, or knees that are shot from twenty years of running," she explains. "It's a different mind-set."

The customers who walked into Yoga U during its first year were older than the young yoga enthusiasts Weese expected, so she quickly adapted her classes to their needs. Because these older people told her they appreciated the deeper levels of yoga, which include breathing exercises to help them relax and reduce stress, she says she began to incorporate more of these elements into her instruction:

> When you get a group of twenty-year-olds, if you try to teach them breath work, or even take a minute in a class to do that, the eyes start rolling. It's different. Whereas the more mature person appreciates it and is interested. For me, the people walking in the door were definitely a much better fit to how I was more comfortable teaching, and wanted to teach, because it was more *me*.

Weese attributes some of Yoga U's success with finding long-term customers to its location in an area with an older population. "I didn't plan it that way, but that's the way it worked out. And I'm really happy about that."

Discovering what customers need is not hard for the operator of a yoga studio. To get instant feedback from her clients, Weese only needs to look out across her studio at her students during class to see if something is working or not.

Set Realistic Expectations

After a successful first year in business, Yoga U was attracting a steady clientele. Weese renewed her lease. She found that she was running a viable business. People were coming back again and again. She had created satisfied repeat customers, who are the bread and butter of any company, large or small.

When trying to judge her success as a yoga studio operator, Weese remembered some good advice she had received years before while attending a yoga training session with a master teacher while she was on vacation from her corporate job:

> One of the teachers that I took a training with, he made a casual comment: "If you can keep one out of ten people coming into your classes, you're doing a really good job." And sure enough, I think his figure was pretty close. Sure enough. That does not sound like a lot, really. I wish you could keep eight out of ten.

Weese has learned to accept a certain level of customer turnover as part of her business. Customers move away, suffer an injury, get pregnant, and change jobs. Sometimes they choose exercise programs that do not include yoga. Weese says that she understands these realities of life that can keep people away from her studio. Nonetheless, the yoga master's words were correct. She says, "I found his number, this one in ten, to be pretty accurate."

Ask, "Should I Stay or Should I Grow?"

After Weese's first year in business, the woman who ran the nail salon next door to her yoga studio decided to close her shop. The landlord asked Weese if she wanted to rent additional space for her studio. At first, she said she didn't want to deal with the extra expense of a larger rent bill every month. She says her husband convinced her otherwise. He reminded her that, as her classes continued to grow, she would need more space. Since her options were either grow now in the space she has, or be forced to move to a completely new location, which might lose customers, she began to share his logic.

Making the decision to grow is tough, especially for a new business. Weese explains, "The financial thing more than doubles when you take on double the space, but the classes didn't support it. So, at that point, I was kind of stressed out." She says she resisted such a big risk after only one year in business. She didn't think she had the experience to make such a big commitment. "It was a very awkward time. I just didn't know what to do." After much consideration and yoga, she chose to grow her business.

After a month of renovations, Yoga U spread into its adjacent space, more than doubling its potential occupancy. After another year in her expanded studio, Weese signed a three-year lease. She says she hesitates before signing every lease: "I still have a problem committing, to be honest. I've always been like that."

Consider Plan B

Weese says she sometimes wonders about her previous life as an employee. She wonders if she is missing out on the long-term security of a corporate job, paid vacations, and a 401k. She says she always comes back to one important truth: "Me, as a person, I definitely connect more with teaching yoga than those things, so that's what keeps me going."

Today, Yoga U is in its seventh year and continues to attract more customers each year. Despite her success, Weese says that a corporate job is still not completely out of the question for her:

> I believe in yoga. I love working in the yoga industry. That's what keeps me going. I'm definitely more of a yoga teacher than I am an administrative assistant, but I would do that. I often tell my husband that's what I'm going to do, and he's like, "Oh no you're not," because he just sees I'm a lot happier now with what I'm doing.

She admits that there are many difficulties in running her own business. "It's really hard for me even to get a night off." Because her business is open seven days a week, she works many hours each week. She teaches six days a week, and she also spends time every day running the business. She says this is one aspect of her work she'd like to improve. "I'm not a real good businessperson, so getting me to do the business stuff is like pulling teeth. That stuff is always backed up." She says that she always gets to it, but it's not her favorite part of having a yoga studio. "It's the teaching yoga that keeps me going, and the doing yoga that keeps me going." The only day Yoga U closes each year is Christmas.

Create Healthy Habits

What is it about yoga that is so appealing to Weese? She explains:

> It just makes you feel so good. It really does. Once you get used to it, and once you start doing yoga, your body just feels better. When you stop, you start to feel bad again. You realize the difference between how a body feels that has a regular yoga practice versus one that doesn't. And not only does it make you feel good, but it is really healthy for your body. It's good for your muscles. It's good for your joints. It's good for your internal organs. It helps. It gives you some peace and quiet time in your head, which we all need. It teaches you things: how to try to breath when you're stressed out. It teaches you these valuable tools that you can really incorporate into your life to make a difference in how you feel physically and mentally.

Weese also loves the fact that yoga is good for everybody, including the elderly. She says, "I see people who have trouble getting up and down off the floor, and I know I'll never be like that."

Do Yoga

Recognizing yoga's salubrious benefits, and its contribution to quality of life, Weese says:

> I do believe everyone should do it. I actually at one point in my life thought that everyone would want to do yoga if they only tried it. That's a very naïve thought, but it's that

kind of thinking that took me to yoga and to opening a yoga studio, just the belief in it, which I still have.

Pick a Style

There are many different variations to yoga, which is essentially a guided exercise involving postures and breathing. With its roots in Hindu culture, ancient yoga was filled with mystical elements involving liberation of the self and union with the universal soul using meditation, postures, and breathing. In Weese's classes, the mystical or religious parts of yoga have been replaced by a physical workout in which clients sweat. To ensure perspiration, Weese and her teachers turn up the heat in the studio before clients arrive.

First clients lay down a mat or two on the polished hardwood floor, then they sit down and stretch. Once the class begins, Weese guides class members through a 90-minute regimen of slow-motion sequential calisthenics, also called a vinyasa. Quiet, instrumental world music plays in the dim room while everyone works up a sweat by holding a variety of poses for short periods of time. If a student gets tired, he or she simply assumes a comfortable "child's pose" until he or she is ready to resume the low-stress workout. After more than an hour, Weese gives class members some relief from the tropical temperatures in the room by handing them a cool lavender-scented washcloth. Finally, the temperature dramatically drops when the doors are opened to let in outside air.

Fans of hot power yoga love its combination of workout and relaxation. Some of these people come back every single day of the week. Although women make up most of Weese's customer base, more than one fourth of her clients are men. And more men are joining every day as they discover the benefits of a regular exercise regimen adorned with a little guided meditation and some mood music.

Know Your Customers

Weese points out that yoga is a very diverse field. "I teach hot power yoga, but I love all yoga. There are many different styles, but the hot power yoga appeals to an individual that has a dedication to fitness." People who like hot power yoga return to classes again and again, which helps to build clientele. Yoga U also offers classes in other, unheated styles of yoga, but they are less popular. Weese says those classes appeal to a different type of person, who typically is not as physically dedicated to a class as a hot power yoga fan. Hot yoga students come back much more often.

"With the hot yoga you get a group of people. They put time in their schedule for their health, for fitness," Weese says. Although she believes in all styles of yoga, and offers a variety of yoga classes, the hot power yoga students are the clients who make her business viable. She says, "It's the hot yoga that keeps the doors open."

Weese explains that the heat actually helps people stretch their muscles deeper and release more toxins while they sweat. But all yoga has many benefits, even for people who don't consider themselves athletes. She says this is part of the reason why she became a yoga instructor:

> In the '70s and '80s, when I was going to yoga classes, you had two kinds of yoga teachers: You had ex-gymnasts who could put both feet around their head, or you had very old people, who would sit for an hour, and you roll your eyes back and forth, and do yoga like that. I kept doing it because I would feel good, even though I knew I couldn't put my feet behind my head. I'll probably never be able to put my feet behind my head.

Although she saw other students move on to other types of fitness programs, Weese kept going to more classes until she began teaching classes. Over the years, she realized she wasn't the only non-ex-gymnast who enjoyed yoga:

> I saw that most people were average people like me. They'll never put the foot behind their head. We may never balance on our pinkies. So I thought, you know what? I relate better to people like this. That's one of the things that led me to teaching yoga. I still believe that most of us will never do this crazy stuff that people tend to think yoga is.

Weese's empathy for people and ability to connect with them are part of her success as a yoga instructor. "I think that's why people like my classes," she says, "because I totally relate to how they're feeling, and to what we can do. We play around, too, with what we can't do, but I try to teach not to get upset about what we can't do, and to have fun with it."

Find Good Employees

Like many self-employed people, Weese says starting her own business was harder than she expected. Finding good employees is one of the hardest parts. Weese says that qualified yoga teachers are hard to get. Over the years, she has discovered the important differences between those who learn from the world's yoga masters and those who are taught in "a teacher training mill" that teaches more about fitness instruction than the valuable depths of yoga. She prefers instructors with real master training, but there is a limited resource. Additionally, she has found it difficult to find people who are available to commit to as many hours per week as she needs. "They want to teach one or two yoga classes a week. It's not like they need this kind of thing. For me, it's my livelihood."

Weese says she responds to customers' needs by putting feedback to work, and sometimes this includes the difficult work of canceling an instructor's class. Ironically, some of her part-time yoga instructors are not as flexible with their time as they are with their bodies. Weese says, "You have to be adaptable and change the schedule based on what's working and what isn't. I'm dealing with this right now. There's a class I have to change because it's just not drawing people in, and the teacher took it very, very personally. It's just hard."

Keep Plugging On

Despite the difficulties, Weese says she is far more satisfied today with her job than she was in her corporate cubicle, and generally much happier. But it's not the best decision she ever made. "The best decision I ever made was marrying my husband. That's the best decision I ever made because he's just an amazing, wonderful person."

She credits her husband, Mark, with much of the success of her business as well as her sense of satisfaction. And she is glad she made the decision to quit her job and start a yoga studio. Although she loves teaching yoga, she says she does not love running a business because she doesn't see herself as a great businessperson. "But," she says, "I love the fact that I actually work in the yoga industry. That makes me happy."

Learn to Adapt

Weese explains:

> Am I happy I did it? Yes. Do I like dealing with the annoyances? No, but I deal with them to try to keep plugging on. And I try to learn from all these things that creep up that I didn't expect. I try to learn from them to not make the same mistakes. I try to learn to adapt.

Weese says her employees have taught her many things about dealing with people and problems. The first time she had a yoga instructor quit, she says it really surprised her. She thought the class was going well, and then the teacher didn't show up for three weeks, forcing Weese to fill in. Then she came into the studio and told Weese she could no longer teach. At first, Weese was freaked out and upset. But she learned to move on. She says:

> I canceled the class. I lost customers, because they were very dedicated to her, but I got over it. So, you deal with a lot of things like that, which have taught me to not get as upset over things as I used to. Do I still get upset? Sure, but nowhere near like I used to.

Although Mark helped Weese immensely in the days leading up to her grand opening, one aspect of her chosen field helped her get her business off the ground in just a few weeks: the low startup costs involved in a yoga studio. "As far as actual startup costs, in comparison to other businesses, it's lower than buying a franchise, which can be $100,000."

Save Money

To save money for her business, Weese does all of her own bookkeeping and housekeeping. Although she doesn't always enjoy these aspects of her business, doing the work herself saves money. She also maintains her business's Web site. She says she would like to make the site nicer by hiring a graphic designer, but she doesn't feel like she can justify the expense. She says, "Yoga is not big business: it's very tough getting people to walk in your door, and things are very out of proportion. What people pay for a yoga class versus what services cost—and this is a very tough part about this business—it's very out of proportion." Since Yoga U is closed most of the day while customers are working or sleeping, she knows there is a limit to the number of hours she can hold classes, and, thus, the number of dollars she can reasonably expect to bring in each week. Therefore, she looks very closely at every expense. She saves money by doing most work herself. Painting the interior of her studio herself was another way she saved money on outside services.

Weese says that, although she advertised during her first two years in business, placing a coupon in local newspapers and magazines did not pay off. "I had two people walk in with the ad for a free yoga class who were already customers! And they wanted their free yoga class." After that, Weese says she decided to forgo advertising. Now she mostly relies on word-of-mouth advertising and referrals—along with her Web site—to draw new customers into her studio.

Get Support and Encouragement

To get a company off the ground, Weese says the main thing that she thinks a new business owner needs is an encouraging spouse or partner. She says she couldn't have done it without the support of her husband. "For me, personally, that's been the biggest help for me, the biggest encouragement, the biggest thing that keeps me going every single day. If somebody has that, it makes your life and doing this so much easier."

Although many small-business owners start with a thoroughly detailed written business plan, Weese says, she did not have one: "I was totally winging everything. But that has been the biggest factor for me, having the support and encouragement of my spouse every single day."

If she could turn back time and change one decision she made along the way to creating her business, Weese says she would have researched the location for her business more because there is another big yoga studio only five miles away. She says if she had the decision to make again today, she would have based her choice of a studio more on location than the cost of rent. She explains,

"At the time, that was what was freaking me out. I should have done more demographic studies, and researched competitors in the area." Recognizing that there are many towns nearby that have no yoga studios at all, she wonders if she might have been more successful farther away from any competition.

On the flipside, Weese knows she's done the best she can with her current location, and feels lucky about many of the other valuable aspects of her current location, such as its proximity to so many great customers who come in every day.

Make People Happy to Be There

Looking into the future, Weese says she knows she will always love working with her wonderful base clientele. Their enthusiasm and friendships help her see herself teaching yoga for the rest of her life. "We've all gotten to know each other and be friends. Those people keep me going. It's just fun to see them. It's fun to do yoga together."

One of the most satisfying aspects of her job is knowing she's helped other people improve their lives through yoga. She says, "It's just such a pleasure when they walk in the door and I can tell they're happy to be there."

Today, Weese Wagner says all of the hard work involved in the adventure to start her own business has improved her life. "The pros definitely outweigh the cons. And I am very blessed and lucky that I have been able to do it, and have had it be working in a manner that my husband and I agree is working. I'm very lucky in that regard. Yes, I can say, it has been worth it."

Top Takeaways

1. Be practical. Don't do anything rash or stupid.

2. Think outside the box. New businesses start when we look past our patterns and reach for distant goals. Often they are closer than we think.

3. Nurture your ideas with formal training. Find an expert and learn everything you can from him or her.

4. Watch for marketplace changes. A shift in the economy or the marketplace can be a great time to establish a niche for your new business.

5. Quit your job when it's time to go. Don't settle for a job that makes you unhappy. Look at your life and decide who you want to be. Don't settle for less.

6. Reach out to a trusted confidant. A spouse, partner, family member, or friend can offer you a different perspective on your situation, which can help you sort things out.

7. Get support. Look realistically around you for the support you need. Being able to ask for support is a strength, not a weakness.

8. Dream big. Look into your heart to find your passions. Don't be afraid to indulge your heart and soul.

9. Go with the flow. When the time is right and all indicators show you have a positive opportunity, research it, make a firm decision, and live it.

10. Tap your resources. Don't waste your resources by ignoring them. Look closely into your relationships to learn their potential to help you succeed.

11. Limit your risk. A part-time job can be the cushion you need to get your business off the ground. Long-term financial obligations can drag you down, so consider all options.

12. Adjust to customers' needs. Your initial vision may need to be tempered by the reality of the marketplace. Stay open to input and feedback from the people who keep you in business.

13. Set realistic expectations. Dream big, but bring your ideas down to earth with advice and feedback from people you trust so you can make them real.

14. Ask, "Should I stay or should I grow?" Too much growth too soon can kill a company without the proper resources, but too little growth can stifle a burgeoning success.

15. Consider Plan B. You don't know what you have until you take time to compare it to what you could have. A backup plan can give you a better sense of Plan A.

16. Create healthy habits. Take care of your mind and body so they can serve you and your business well for many years to come.

17. Do yoga. Low-stress exercise, peaceful meditation, and habitual fitness can help you live a longer and happier life. Also, stretching out prevents injuries. Start slow, but keep at it.

18. Pick a style. Once you know who you are, challenge yourself by exploring other areas that might fit you differently and perhaps better.

19. Know your customers. Read your customers every day. Incorporate feedback into your plan.

20. Find good employees. This might be the hardest part of your business, but it is worth the effort.

21. Keep plugging on. Don't let setbacks keep you down. Sometimes owning a business is rough. Keep an eye on what makes you happy.

22. Learn to adapt. Change is inevitable, especially when you are trying to make a better life for yourself. Practice your flexibility wherever it is needed.

23. Save money. A little savings can go a long way when you're just starting out. Doing jobs yourself can save you extra expenses.

24. Get support and encouragement. Don't do it alone. Surround yourself with the people who make you feel good about yourself.

25. Make people happy to be there. Listen to customers, learn what thrills them, and then give it to them. Happy customers come back, and repeat customers keep you afloat.

Chapter 7

Why Work for Yourself?

freelancer n. *a writer or artist who is independent of long-term contracts but works for individual customers under short-term contracts*

Entrepreneurs see opportunities wherever they emerge. Many of these opportunities come in the form of knowledge, money, or relationships. A steady flow of opportunities can provide a new business owner with the necessary income to create a thriving business.

Often, the opportunities available for a full-time freelancer are unavailable for those already working full time for corporate employers because their job responsibilities create overpowering time and deadline constraints. Outsourced project work often goes to those independent business owners who spend their days juggling various projects while working from their home offices simply because they are there when they are needed. Today, as more large companies send work outside their walls, freelance work is flourishing, creating more opportunities for full-time freelancers.

Although many freelancers rely on the Internet and its abundant commercial sources of freelance work, others build their clientele through relationships established and grown through many e-mails, phone conversations, and face-to-face meetings. When freelance writer Chris Murray quit his job three years ago, he was able to start a freelance writing operation immediately thanks to an influx of large writing projects from contacts he had created and nurtured while working in the publishing industry for more than a decade.

CHRIS MURRAY, 50—FREELANCE WRITER

I met Chris Murray while I was toiling away for our mutual employer. I was slumped in my cubicle in a windowless part of a giant room; Chris was slumped in his office on the edge of that giant room, enjoying the view from his window, but not his thankless job. During that time, one of the best parts of my job was working with Chris, who eventually became my manager. As a mentor, he taught me how to do a job he had done for many years. One day, after a long history with the company, Chris got fed up with his job and quit. The day he gave his two weeks notice, a smile appeared on his face that continues to brighten his whole life.

The company was left scrambling when he quit. Reacting to the crisis, my boss hastily threw an overdue raise at me to keep up my good work. I was also told I would not receive the resources needed to do the job properly. Realizing that I was the only person left in the building with the institutional knowledge needed to create the company's main product, I saw my opportunity for independence. I revised a plan I had been concocting for months, and quit the following week. I turned in a letter of resignation, consisting of my two weeks notice and a short letter thanking my boss for the wonderful opportunities the company had given me. Before panic and resentment set in, I next handed my soon-to-be former employer a price list for the services I could provide the company as an independent contractor. My relationship with my former employer proved its strength and held fast. We both confirmed that we would like to continue to work together as contractor and customer rather than employee and boss. Offering lower prices than my competitors, as well as an intimate knowledge of the product I learned from Chris, I started my own business and procured my first big customer. As they say, I couldn't have done it without him.

Tap Professional and Personal Relationships

Chris says that the opportunity to quit his job and start his own business came from the professional and personal relationships he had created and sustained with the book publishers with whom he worked while in his job:

> I developed relationships in the industry, so I could use these relationships. These are people who knew me. They knew that I was a writer, and that I could write. We got along personally—professionally and personally—and I could use them as sources of work. It was a win–win relationship: They had use of my services, and I could get the jobs from them.

As a person who works with books for a living, Chris says one book that helped him prepare for becoming self-employed was *Creating You and Company* by author and consultant William Bridges. In his book, Bridges writes that conventional jobs are no longer the best way to get work done, and encourages people to find their appropriate "lifework." He also promotes the idea of looking for opportunity in change, maximizing the potential of personal desire, and learning to "think like the CEO of your own career."

Chris explains that when he started, he had a marketing plan, which included a direct mailing to book publishers to let them know that he was available as a full-time freelance writer and editor. Before he could put it into action, his plan became obsolete because a potential customer suddenly asked him if he was available to help write a book. Chris says, "I told them, 'Well, the timing's perfect because actually I'm going to become a full-time freelancer, so yes!'"

Industry connections brought Chris his first customer as a self-employed freelancer. Then other clients offered him work. Today, three years later, Chris' full-time freelancing business has grown simply from word-of-mouth marketing. He explains: "I never put up a Web site, which I intended to do, and I still intend to do it some time if I ever have time. I've never even put business cards together, and in my situation I really should have a business card to give, but as far as marketing, I haven't done anything."

Make Your Move

Part of the impetus for Chris to get his business off the ground was a solid nest egg of savings. In addition, his wife, Donna, has a full-time job as a library administrator, which includes health care benefits for her husband and children. Steady freelance work has kept Chris from having to fall back on his Plan B. "I've been lucky enough to make money from the get-go, so we haven't had to tap into our savings."

Every new entrepreneur should have a safety net to prevent any kind of financial hardship from a business. Chris says that savings is how he was able to take the big risk of quitting his job and starting his own. In fact, he says, he and his wife are very risk-averse, "more than you should be if you're going to be an entrepreneur." But suddenly, his backup plan fell into place, so he decided to make the jump:

> We wanted more than just a year of savings, because we have kids and college coming up. This was not a good time to make the plunge, but there was this windfall. As it turns out, we haven't had to use it. Most people are not going to have that luxury. We're not really entrepreneurial in spirit, because we are so risk averse. We are the kinds of people who would never quit a job before having another job.

Chris says that having money in his savings account reduced the risk of quitting his job to become a freelancer, but his many contacts in the publishing industry also helped seal the deal. Plus, the overhead of a freelancer who works from home is extremely low compared with most industries.

> This was about the least risky entrepreneurial jump you can imagine. I mean, between the "no overhead," between the windfall, between the savings we already had, between my wife's job, which was enough for a good salary, we got to about six safety nets before we took the plunge.

Before all these security measures were in place, he says he had not envisioned himself as the owner of a small business.

Get Organized

Chris says that one of the most important things he has learned over the past few years as a freelancer is the value of self-organization. He advises new entrepreneurs to get very organized. He says, "Follow your expenses with spreadsheets, and know every day what's just come in." He says he has learned the importance of managing a budget, especially when tax time rolls around:

> I keep everything, but I pick the wrong time to tally it up. Stay on top of expenses. Luckily, my expenses are Post-its, reams of paper, little things like that. If I was running a store, I would have been under a tidal wave. This entrepreneurial adventure is probably the simplest, least risky one. And clearly, thankfully it is, because I would have drowned!

While knocking on wood, Chris explains that finding work as a freelance writer is actually easier than he thought it would be: "So far, that's been the easy part. The tough part is staying organized and making efficient use of your time, especially when you have kids." Chris points out that it's very easy to get involved with the activities of a busy family when working from home. He says, "You can be involved in all the activities, you just have to be efficient."

Beyond his safety nets for security, Chris quit his job because he was unhappy with its prospects for his future. After twelve years, he hit a ceiling from which he saw little chance of promotion, more money, or career growth. In addition, he found parts of his job unsatisfying, such as contract negotiations, which he saw as an area of weakness. Focusing on his many strengths rather than his weaknesses, Chris has made his business a success from the start.

Make Personal Improvements

Like many other entrepreneurs, Chris Murray says that starting his own business was a wise choice. "Besides marrying my wife, I would say it's the best decision I ever made, absolutely: on a professional level, absolutely, and actually, on a personal level as well."

When Chris quit his job in March 2006 to work as a freelancer, his son was in sixth grade and his daughter was just starting high school. He found that working from home allowed him to help both of his active children with their many projects and events. The flexibility of working from home also helped him relieve his wife of much of the burden of driving their children around throughout the week. The timing was right. "She had gotten a promotion, and was less available to do the things she had done before," he says. "Personally, it worked out great, where I could pick up the slack."

The working situation in which Chris found himself actually mirrored my own transition to working from home in many ways. When I quit my job, my wife was free to move from her part-time position to a full-time role, in which she has prospered and grown professionally. My freelancing job enabled her to capitalize on opportunities that would have been impossible for her to take if I had continued to work in a job that kept me away from home five days per week.

Get Paid

Chris admits he made a few mistakes along the way to getting his business off the ground, which have taught him many important lessons about having his own freelance business. While professing the importance of better recordkeeping and better time management, he says he learned one other valuable lesson in his first year of self-employment:

> Get paid. Get paid for your work. I did things on spec, and I spent hundreds of hours, and got nothing. It's not that people were trying to take advantage of me. They believed what I believed: that we would put something together and then sell it, and then we would get paid. But the trouble is, it took much, much longer to do, and then it didn't sell, and then boom, there's no money. So, get paid for everything you do. If you're going to write a book proposal, get a fee for it. If you are going to do something, always get paid for your time.

While he does some editing work for a publisher at an hourly rate, most of his significant projects are based on a flat fee negotiated at the beginning of the project. Much like my own business, Chris's freelance business has around three or four primary clients who allow him to make a living as a self-employed writer and editor. Sometimes he gets so swamped with work that he needs to delay a new project, but he never turns down jobs because he is too busy.

Have Realistic Expectations

As a business writer with decades of experience in the publishing industry, Chris says he had a pretty good idea about what he was getting himself into when he quit. He says he enjoys many aspects of working alone, away from the corporate environment. "I thought that I would love not having to commute; I still love not having to commute," Chris says, "It's been two years. I still like to listen to the radio traffic knowing that I don't have to deal with it!"

Make Logical Moves

Years of experience inside an industry can give a new business owner the skills and knowledge he or she needs to quit a job and start a company. A deep base of practical, hands-on knowledge and focused talent can create a solid foundation for realistic confidence. "You don't start a business if you don't think that you have a very good chance of succeeding." Chris says he simply made a logical move in his industry:

> I just basically went to another part of the industry, but I used the same skill. I was writing a newsletter about business books, so I was a writer and an editor about books, and the business book industry, of course, needs writers of books. So there was a very logical move from one to the other. It's almost like the professional football player becoming the assistant coach. It's the same industry. It's logical. That also made it safe. It was a very safe move.

One investment Chris made at the outset of his business was the purchase of a new Mac laptop computer. After a year of working in the guest bedroom of his house, he made a second large investment in his company's infrastructure by having his basement converted into a comfortable office space. "And I still manage to be disorganized," he jokes. "Can you imagine if I had inventory?"

Manage Your Time Well

Chris says his empty house during the day is a great place to work. "I usually work from 8 A.M. to 3 P.M., with a break for lunch. When the kids get home, it gets a little complicated, driving them around and stuff like that. The days are a little short." On his current assignment, he says he starts work at 7 A.M. Under a tighter deadline, he'll start as early as 5 A.M. He says his schedule changes day by day, and he'll occasionally work weekends or late at night if a project requires more hours. He adds, "If I'm under deadline pressure, then I just tell my family, 'I've got to get this done. I'll be working Saturday.'"

To create more family time away from home, Chris says he tries to set aside a few weeks every year for a family vacation. Although he says he often starts a vacation with grand notions of completing work while he is away from home, this often does not work out as planned. "I usually take my laptop on vacation; I rarely open it."

Risk Is Relative

There are many benefits that come along with quitting your job and starting your own business. Some people believe that staying in a company can actually be more risky for your personal life and professional career than starting your own job because self-employment can often provide a better sense of permanence than a job for someone else who could downsize your job or ship it overseas.

Now that the "loyalty contract" between companies and their employees that was common many years ago has almost been completely replaced by job instability and uncertainty, sometimes it becomes a question of not whether you can afford to quit your job and start your own business, but whether you can afford *not* to quit your job and start your own company. Every entrepreneur must choose for him or herself the level of risk that is realistic for his or her personal, professional, financial, and family circumstances.

Chris says he has never regretted the decision to take the risk to quit his job and start his own. He adds, "I'm happy."

Top Takeaways

1. Tap professional and personal relationships. Maintaining professional and personal connections in your industry while working for others can pay off when you quit.

2. Make your move. If your financial situation suddenly undergoes a positive change, use the leeway to make a positive change in your work situation.

3. Get organized. Manage your budget and keep track of all profits, expenses, customers, and suppliers.

4. Make personal improvements. Weigh all of your options, personal and professional, when making a decision to change work scenarios. Don't neglect one for the other.

5. Get paid. Favors can help you earn new customers, but paid work is what keeps a business going. Ken Blanchard, the management guru, points out that if you're not getting paid for the work you do, it's a hobby, not a profession.

6. Have realistic expectations. Don't let the stars in your eyes blind you to the reality of supply and demand.

7. Make logical moves. Once you've gained valuable experience in your industry, find ways to move up and become more independent.

8. Manage your time well. Pay close attention to your calendar and clock so you can meet all of your deadlines. The flexibility of self-employment takes a dedicated effort to form a productive schedule.

Chapter 8

How to Meet People Who Can Help You Start a Business

networking n. *to create connections and share information with other people in an informal setting, while pursuing a career*

Sometimes getting out into public is the best strategy for creating the foundation on which to base your dream of self-employment. Getting out of your daily grind and meeting others in your community can create the relationships that help make a business venture a reality. Many entrepreneurs create their businesses from a few key connections to the people around them who help them turn their visions into reality. They create viable companies out of networks of people and their common supply and demand. Online connections can work, too, but personal, face-to-face meetings are the most powerful tools in a new business owner's tool belt.

One entrepreneur who benefited from a chain of chance encounters while out on the town is Jerad Schaffer, an entrepreneur who started his business in March 2006 after leaving his former employer and industry to enter new career territory: He bought a bar and transformed it into a music mecca. Nearly three years later, he continues to succeed as his own boss in the vibrant social world of nighttime entertainment.

JERAD SHAFFER, 35—NIGHTCLUB OWNER

For many years after I moved away from California—a state where music is plentiful and well appreciated—I lamented the fact that there were no venues near my home in Delaware that featured regular, original, local live music. One day, a few years ago, my hopeful desires were fulfilled when an old dive bar up the street from my house was suddenly transformed from the low-key Brandywine Tavern, known locally as either Nick's or Sneaky Pete's, into Mojo 13. Suddenly, an old biker bar that rarely featured live entertainment became the center of a thriving, local, live music scene.

When I went to investigate, I learned that a new entrepreneur and his girlfriend partnered with the owner of the bar, redesigned the interior to reflect their interests in circus sideshow themes, and began featuring live music and entertainment almost every night of the month. Their hard work created a lively hub of creative nighttime excitement and activity, as well as a haven for all types of musicians and their fans. Even the big daily newspaper, *The News Journal*, seemed to embrace the club and its hip young owners with ravenous coverage. The bar became a quick success. The revitalization of the area's live music scene has paralleled the rejuvenation of the bar from standard saloon to remarkable entertainment venue, located strangely in the middle of suburban Wilmington, Delaware, on Philadelphia Pike on the way to lovely downtown Claymont.

As a fan of live, original music, I have frequented Mojo 13 with friends often since it opened. Over that time, I have become friends with the man who started the club after he left his former career as a corporate graphic designer and started down a more independent path.

Before his current profession, Jerad was working full time for one of the largest magazines in the country retouching photos. Although he was using the degree in graphic design he earned from Penn State University in 1994, he wasn't satisfied in his corporate workstation. He was ready for a new direction.

Explore What You Want and Connect with Others Who Want the Same

Jerad confesses that he had spent ten years avoiding using his college degree. "I used it for personal stuff, and it did help me get certain jobs that were related to graphics, but I never really got a 'graphics design' job." At the magazine job, Jerad was originally hired for the graveyard shift in the prepress department, preparing ads for print. That job turned into a regular day job that involved similar Photoshop skills and graphic design tasks. Eventually, his daily job involved retouching photographs and other prepress print shop prep work. Although he had a media industry employer, Jerad says he was unsatisfied. He was still searching for his dream job.

As a musician and art lover, Jerad needed more creativity in his job but settled for a boring art job because it paid the bills. Although he had gone to school for graphic design, his heart was not really in it. He says art school taught him that a career in graphic design was not what he wanted to do with the rest of his life. "I was so burnt out on it that I just wanted to be in a rock band; that's what I wanted to do. I realized it even when I went into college."

After college, Jerad worked in Boscov's department store. Like many graduates, he was still unsure of his career path. He says he had no desire at that time to use his degree, because he needed a break after many intense years engulfed in graphic design. Instead, he found a steady job that offered him the money and spare time with which he could pursue his desire to rock on the side.

Jerad explains that the time working in retail was well spent. Not only did he learn some essential business and customer skills that would help him launch his own business, but he also met his fiancée, Gretchen Gatchel, who played a large role in his decision to start his own business. Coincidentally, Gretchen also attended Penn State at the same time as Jerad, although they never met. Her degree was in education, but like Jerad, she was working in a department store rather than working in the field of her degree. Once they met, she became the guitarist in his band, Sissy Mary, which soon became She/He.

Make Things More Effective

Jerad says that his career was in a holding pattern that he wanted to break:

> I was basically working at [the company] doing that, and still trying to figure out what I was going to do with my life, some sort of pursuit. I just didn't want to be there. I was there for five years. They continued to downsize that whole time period. We just kept getting smaller and smaller. Our department went from being ten people to being three or four people when I left. Just the way that technology has changed and the way that readership's gone, [my employer was] facing tough times, too. They were trying to figure out how to revamp their business and make things more effective.

Now that he owns his own business, Jerad says he understands his former employer's position as a business owner better than ever. He adds that the same economics apply to his own bar: "The saving grace is trying to figure out how to keep your expenses down."

Even while he worked as a salesperson at Boscov's, he was pursuing another interest in a different industry: antiques. For years, he had been learning about antiques from his parents, who helped him appreciate the skills of a professional antiques dealer. Jerad says he still uses the skills he learned from his early experiences with his parents while continuing to sell antiques as a side business. He says he has always been interested in finding bargains, so many of his days have been spent in auctions and antiques stores. When he is antiquing, he likes to find the wild, three-ring circus decorations with which he enjoys decorating his life.

Shop around for What You Love

Jared says he honed many of the business skills he uses today while working in the world of antiques. As a boy, he started going to flea markets and thrift shops. As an adult, he became adept at buying and selling at auctions. He says these interests led to his involvement in his first small business venture:

I'd spent so many hours at auctions, I started realizing, well, I could sell stuff on the side on eBay or in antiques shops. So I started doing that. I had an antiques shop for a year. I had met other people my age who would go to auctions as well. We opened up a shop in Downingtown [Pennsylvania], but that's a very tough business.

After several months running an antiques shop, Jerad and his partners mutually decided to close the business. Despite the store's sad demise, Jerad says he still had his eyes open for another type of self-employment opportunity, even while working for a big company. He says he wanted to do something he loves:

Anything you do, what you've got to do, you should do something you love. I do love the antiques business, but the thing I like most is going to the auctions. I don't like having a shop, or sitting there on my weekends, just sitting there in the shop. That aspect of it isn't what got me into it. That's not what grabs me about it. I like being able to go out and just travel to different auctions. You just never know what you're going to see. You're just always looking for that, "Ooh, I found one of these for a great price." You just never know. There's just sort of this quest. That's what I enjoyed about it.

After closing the antiques shop, Jerad's unsatisfying full-time job filled his days while he tried to figure out what to do next. As he watched layoffs increase at his company, he knew his time to leave was imminent. Although he was not satisfied with his job, he continued to work there, thinking about alternative employment plans while waiting for the axe to fall.

Save Money to Survive

One day, at the end of the summer, Jerad took a rare vacation day to go to the beach. While enjoying the sun and surf, he received a call on his cell phone from a friend at work. The friend relayed bad news from the boss: Jerad and several other employees in his department would be laid off in two months.

Sometimes a life-changing phone call can come out of the blue. While he was away from his work, enjoying himself with his fiancée at the beach, his company's leaders had gathered their employees together in the lunchroom to inform everyone who would be leaving in October. Jerad's name was on the list.

He says this news from the office helped him because it pushed him into a better part of his career adventure. Undisturbed by the inevitable news, Jerad says he welcomed the impetus to change his life. His biggest concern was the startup costs of a new venture, and choosing which interest he was going to pursue with that venture. He says:

> The toughest thing about getting involved with something else was just figuring out, how can I get something started up? How can I get into something else but still have money to survive during that time? Do I have the savings, or what do I have to do to make that happen? Sometimes I guess that's the toughest thing or the most deterring thing to people. Even now, I look at it like, if I was to open another bar or something, where do I come up with the capital to do that, and how many months do I have to pay rent and do all this stuff just to get the thing off the ground? How far do I have to go into debt before I can even open the doors?

Consider Your Options

Jerad says being faced with an imminent layoff from his corporate job helped him finally seriously consider his next big career move. He says he wasn't ready to just fall into another corporate job so he could continue to pay his mortgage. With a severance package and unemployment benefits, he had the financial resources to contemplate his next step forward. He decided to pursue his passion for antiques by getting more involved. He says, "At that time I was like, well here's my opportunity to become an auctioneer."

Because Pennsylvania requires antiques auctioneers to be licensed, Jerad took the required classes for several months. When other students asked him whether he planned to open an auction house like them, he said he replied, "Yeah, that would be kind of cool, but I'd really like to open a bar." But a bar still seemed like a distant dream, because Jerad's only experience in the nightclub industry was his role as a band member booking shows and playing in local bars. He says, "I had no idea what you do to open a bar."

Get Help

Once he began to look into the possibility of opening his own place, Jerad realized he needed help. Although he thinks of himself as a very independent type of person, he eagerly sought advice. He says:

> It's nice to know and to find people who know more than you about certain things. Or, if there are things you're not interested in doing, you need to find those people who are better at that or interested in doing that sort of thing, and make those kinds of connections, relationships, and friend-ships and partnerships.

Building networks is one of Jerad's strengths, so he used his ability to connect with others to get started. While looking for the capital to get a bar off the ground, he hit a big roadblock: He had never worked in a bar before. He was starting a bar from scratch.

Around the time his auctioneer courses ended, Jerad's severance pay and unemployment benefits began to dwindle. He faced the prospect of getting another corporate job. He says his future was looking bleak: Temp agencies were offering him corporate jobs. He says, "I was just like, 'Oh my God. I don't want to do that.'"

Although Jerad had income from buying and selling antiques, he was ready for a drastic change. He had to do something new. Once he had his auctioneer's license in hand, his options included learning how to start an auction house, or simply working harder to hustle antiques as a full-time job. Jerad says, "My heart really was still thinking, 'well, that's kind of cool, but I'd still like to have a bar.'"

Besides his inexperience, another hurdle Jerad faced was the fact that there was no bar near his house that he was interested in buying. He says he didn't see any bar in Delaware that was like the live music venues he enjoyed in nearby Philadelphia. He wanted his bar to reflect a style that was unheard of in suburban Delaware where he lived: old-time circus sideshow.

Make Your Mistakes Worthwhile

Jerad looks at his decision to start his own business philosophically. He explains:

> There are people who say, "You get dealt a certain hand in life," and I'll always say, "You know, there are mistakes you make. What you have to do is end up where you want to be, so it makes all those mistakes worthwhile."

While he was still going to auctioneer school, Jerad was also searching eBay at night for possible bar locations. He was also conducting research on bars by enjoying the nightlife in Philadelphia. One night in Philly, Jerad and Gretchen met several important people who would lead them to Mojo 13.

Set a Chain of Events into Motion

A random chain of rock-and-roll events led Jerad to a show at a bar near his home in Delaware, where he met a valuable ally in his search for a new career in entertainment. During the show at the Crerand, a guy around Jerad's age came over to his table with a pitcher of beer and started a casual conversation. Jerad soon learned that this guy, Jeff McKay, owned the Crerand, and they quickly became friends. He also met Andrew Miller, who had booked the show that night and now helps Jerad book shows for Mojo 13.

In a single night, Jerad's interest in finding a venue for his rock band helped him make several crucial connections that would become valuable in his new business venture. During their initial conversation, Jeff mentioned his other bar, Sneaky Pete's, which is located only a few blocks away. Jerad had never heard of the bar because it rarely featured live music.

Several weeks later, when they met again at a bar in Philadelphia, Jeff offered Jerad the job of booking bands at Sneaky Pete's. Jerad told Jeff, "Well, I really don't want to just book bands at some venue unless I can have some sort of input into the décor and everything and just be able to go in 100 percent." Ideas for his new business were taking shape. "I still didn't really have an idea that it was going to be like this," he adds, motioning to the circus atmosphere inside today's Mojo 13.

Recognize Opportunities

Many months later, after leaving his job and meeting the people who might be able to help him start his own job, Jared called Jeff to ask him, "How do you open a bar?" Jeff answered him with the question, "Do you want to buy a bar? I'll sell you half of Sneaky Pete's." Suddenly, Jerad had the very real prospect of a business on his hands. He liked the possibility of taking an existing bar and reworking it into his own vision of a cool entertainment venue.

Jeff owned the business with a partner, but he wanted somebody else to take over his partner's half of the business. He told Jerad that Sneaky Pete's was just basically staying afloat. Although the bar was paying its bills, it was not realizing its fullest potential. Jeff also told Jerad that the bar's most successful nights were the nights when bands played.

Jerad says he was surprised by Jeff's proposition. "At first, I went from walking around two days before thinking, 'What am I going to do?' And then, all of a sudden, it's like, 'If you come up with this amount of money, there you go: You have a bar.'"

Consider Startup Costs

Jerad says the financial commitment was formidable, but within the realm of possibility. Jeff's partner wanted a reasonable price, which was close to a year's salary at Jerad's former job. He says he looked at the investment like it was less than the startup costs of starting from square one. The small investment was cheaper than buying or building a bar and getting together all the paperwork and licenses a new bar requires. By buying half of Jeff's business, he could become self-employed while skipping all of the hassles building a bar from nothing entails. Plus, from Day 1, he would be making money from the bar's current customer base.

Jerad considered the deal for a few days, added some money he borrowed from his parents to money from his savings, and bought Jeff's partner's half of the business.

Jerad named the new business venture Mojo 13, which soon became Delaware's premier live original music venue.

Jerad says he couldn't have started his business without help from his parents, who he feels very lucky to have: "My parents have always been very encouraging for me to do anything I want to do. My parents are very supportive." Thanks to his strong relationship with his parents, he was able to pursue his dream of self-employment in his chosen field. "I think they just looked at it like, "Hey. Go for it. Pay us back whenever you can."

Jerad took over as the bar's manager, backup bartender, and day-to-day operator. Within a few days, he started renovations on the building's interior and exterior, including the construction of a 20-foot clown's face with glowing red eyes hovering above the front door to greet patrons and neighbors.

While the bar was still getting up and running, Jerad says he paid his bills with tips from bartending, a job in which he became more skilled every day. By summer 2006, Mojo 13 was earning a positive reputation as a notable spot on the musical map. Many bands were coming from across the country and the world to perform. For almost three years now, the bar has provided Jerad with a comfortable income.

Still, Jerad says, he's not finished. There are still many things that he wants to do that he hasn't done yet. He says that he will eventually turn Mojo 13 into the perfect bar of his dreams, but it might take a few more years. This type of approach is part of his personality. He explains, "That's one of my shortcomings. I'd say I'm very deliberate about stuff, but also sometimes very slow about it."

Consider the Tradeoffs

Jerad says there are always tradeoffs you make when you work for yourself, but he finds it more satisfying than working for other people:

> When I used to have my day job, I went to my day job, I came home, and I didn't bring it home at all. That's one thing I liked about it. It wasn't necessarily rewarding, it wasn't what I went to school for, but at least when I worked there, I got paid, it didn't kill me, and I came home and did what I wanted to do. Now, I have more free time, and I have the luxury of being able to hang out with Gretch, but I get calls at 10:00 at night saying that this is blowing up, or somebody got punched in the parking lot, or we're out of this, could you get this? Or, a band cancelled, or who's here doing this? It just sort of became 24/7, but I still have free time.

Nonetheless, Jerad says he still prefers owning a bar to his old day job. "It's more of what I really like. It's definitely more satisfying."

Jerad says running his own business also teaches him many management and business skills that he will always have for the future. He has also learned more about booking bands than most booking agents. His experiences as a bar owner who books live shows have introduced him to an entirely new business vocabulary of contracts, guarantees, advances, proximity clauses, riders, and logistics.

Meet People
Jerad says owning a business has taught him something else:

> The one thing I've learned, and the one thing that took me a while to learn that I wish I'd have known better or had done more when I was younger was, get out and meet people. Meet people who are doing what you enjoy. Meet people who are successful at what you enjoy doing, or what you want to be, and try to learn from them. Try to just be involved. Definitely, a lot of times it's who you know. It's who you know, and then a lot of times, what you know is from who you know. How you learn it is from doing, just being involved and getting out there.

Live Your Vision
With Jerad at its helm, Mojo 13 has become an important local employer with a tight-knit workforce and customer base that often overlap. Jerad's vision for his business was to create opportunities for people like himself, and to surround himself with people from whom he could learn as well.

Jerad has learned many lessons that apply to his life as a musician and business owner from the many people with whom he works. Owning a bar and starting a business have helped him pay his bills while also keeping him involved in creating a vibrant local music scene that he loves every day. He says he gets great satisfaction from being connected with "other people who have the same sort of dreams and the same sort of visions, and the same sort of interest."

Like many self-employed business owners, Jerad says he really should do more marketing, especially because he is a professional graphic designer. He admits that he still has not printed a business card for himself, nor created a mailing list. On the other hand, the design work on the outside and inside of his business is remarkable for any live music venue, especially in the suburbs of Wilmington, and always gets people's attention. In addition, thanks to his many friends in the community and the media, Jerad's club is featured regularly in the local mainstream and underground press. Although he still has yet to create the perfect Web site, his MySpace page is a popular way his customers connect to the latest information about his club's future performances, events, and artists. It also lets customers sample songs from upcoming bands and provides Jerad with a free promotional tool that keeps his network updated and growing.

He says his latest priority is getting the word out about shows. He laments, "I wish I had taken by now more steps to make that easier on myself."

Take Care of One Another

One business benefit of Jerad's social behavior and love of people is the loyal and reliable crew of staff members who help him and his partner Jeff make their business a success. Most of the people he has hired have stayed with him over the past two years. He explains that his employees stay because he really cares about them. "We're very loyal. That's what we're hoping for."

He says his secret to hiring people is finding individuals who value teamwork:

> If we hire somebody, we're just hoping for somebody you can trust, and who is looking out for the bar, and looking out for the team. That's the thing I hope. That's how we try to treat people. We're going to look out for you and try to take care of you as best we can. As far as bartenders, or whoever, we just try to make them as much money as possible. And vice versa. We're just hoping for that.

Top Takeaways

1. Explore what you want and connect with others who want the same. Talk with people wherever you go about your dreams and desires for the future. Some of them might have what you need to get started.

2. Make things more effective. Look for ways to cut costs and prevent waste. Develop habits that save money, energy, resources, and so on. Sustainability is key.

3. Shop around for what you love. Once you know what makes you happy, find ways to pursue it for a profit.

4. Save money to survive. Don't ever leave yourself in a desperate situation. Explore ways to gather the capital it takes to get a business off the ground.

5. Consider your options. Spend time considering what you like and do not like about your career, then take steps to get more of what you like while eliminating the negatives.

6. Get help. Nobody can go it alone. Helping others is a great way to start a mutually beneficial relationship. Nurture relationships you might need in the future.

7. Make your mistakes worthwhile. Turn your mistakes into learning experiences with vast rewards. Nobody moves forward without stumbling a few times.

8. Set a chain of events into motion. Once things get moving, keep pushing to build momentum. Large efforts early in the life of a business pay off in the long run.

9. Recognize opportunities. Seriously consider unexpected offers that fall into your lap. Don't act recklessly, but don't pass up on a rare chance to plot a path to your dreams.

10. Consider startup costs. Gather the resources you will need to get your business up and running, and then get more because startup costs are always higher than you think.

11. Consider the tradeoffs. Sometimes working for somebody else is a far better way to advance your career and find satisfaction than working for yourself. Other times it is not.

12. Meet people. Get out and mingle. Learn to read people. Schmooze a little. But don't act like a jerk. Find people who share your dream by sharing it with them.

13. Live your vision. Making your vision known to others encourages them to find their own. Once you've found your vision, help other people find their vision.

14. Take care of each other. Hiring employees is a great way to support the people in your community who support you. Make friends by showing people you care about them.

Chapter 9

How to Succeed with Your People

self-actualization n. *the reaching and achievement of a person's fullest potentials, goals, skills, talents, etc.*

After graduating from high school, Delaware native Richard Cherrin joined the Navy, where he served for four years. With money from the GI Bill, he left the service and got his bachelor's degree in psychology and sociology. After graduation, he took a job as a counselor at the Department of Labor. With an aptitude for working with people and business systems, he moved into management. Mid-level management jobs turned into a top white-collar corporate executive position in the health care industry thanks to his seasoned business acumen and a master's of business administration degree from Central Michigan University, where he majored in operations research and management.

RICHARD CHERRIN, 67—BUSINESS TEACHER/FORMER CEO

After many years as a manager in the health care industry, Richard became the CEO of the Visiting Nurses Association (VNA), a successful home-care provider. At VNA, he used entrepreneurial strategies to expand the company from two office locations employing fewer than 100 nurses and other health care professionals to thirteen locations employing more than 1,300 health care professionals. When he started, annual revenues for the company were less than $1 million. When he retired in 2001, the company's revenue base exceeded $39 million. Now retired, he spends his days helping business students and business owners get started by teaching part time at the local community college and consulting on the side. Richard's success in both academic and business realms has taught him many important lessons about creating and nurturing the human relationships needed to build a business. As a business leader, teacher, and consultant, he offers many valuable tips and insights about hiring and managing the people who keep a business alive and growing.

Recognize Self-Interest

When new business owners are ready to grow by hiring employees, Richard says they can learn an important lesson from Scottish philosopher and economist Adam Smith, who lived in the days when the United States fought for and won its independence from Great Britain:

> Adam Smith was talking about self-interest. If you want to work with people, if you want to be successful with people, what you have to do is find out what is in their self-interest. What do they need? What are they trying to accomplish? If you can find out what someone else is trying to accomplish, and you can provide that for them, there is nothing, I mean there's *nothing*, you can't have. Determine what their self-interest is, what's their need, and meet it, including your employees. What does your employee need? That's what Adam Smith was talking about when he said, "It is not from the benevolence of the butcher, the brewer, or the baker, that we expect our dinner, but from their regard to their own self-interest. We address ourselves, not to their humanity but to their self-love, and never talk to them of our own necessities but of their advantages."
>
> We don't speak to them of our needs. We speak to them about their own self-interest and their self-love. It's really amazing.

Richard says keeping this in mind has helped him succeed in his career and life: Find out how you and your people can make each other successful. To do this, he told his direct reports that to become successful themselves, they needed to help him succeed at satisfying his board of directors. When they made him look good in front of his peers, he worked hard to make them look good in front of their peers. He says, "That's how it works."

Richard believes that asking people works better than telling them. When helping employees become more productive, managers need to ask their employees what they need from management. This dialogue should take place before management assumes an employee's motivations. Richard explains, "This philosophy can extend to all aspects of an entrepreneur's business, including sales, marketing, employees, networking, and management."

In sales, this type of economic philosophy has been called *permission marketing*. In management and leadership, some experts call it *360-degree leadership*. Both business processes rely on the same valuable communication strategy, which involves asking people questions and getting to know people and their needs first before trying to sell to them or tell them what they need to do.

Ask Questions About People's Needs

Richard says he saw this way of thinking in action recently when he helped his daughter buy a new car from a salesperson who embraced the philosophy of discovering people's self-interest for mutual benefit:

> I was there during the three interactions they had together. I said, "Val, we can do better pricing at this point. Now we have all the information we need, we can price it better."
>
> She said, "No, Dad, I don't want to do that. I want to buy from this guy."
>
> He sold himself, and Val needed to buy from this guy. Even if she may have saved a thousand bucks, she wasn't willing to do that. From his first conversation when we went out for a drive, he was trying to find out from Val what she needed in a car, what she needed in her life.

The salesman who sold the car to Val never gave her a sales pitch. He simply connected with her by asking her questions about herself and her needs. That's why the salesperson has been successful in his job for more than twenty-seven years. He simply served as the person and resource she needed to help her buy her new car, which is exactly what she needed at that moment. Richard explains, "She needed a guy who she trusted, and she had a good sense about him. I was thinking, okay, let's go online. You've gotten the technical assistance, now let's go online and buy the car."

Instead of taking her father's advice to look elsewhere for the car, Val acted on her personal feelings and bought the car from the salesman who asked questions and listened to what she needed. She felt it was worth the $1,000 she might have saved elsewhere to give this person her business. Richard says he backed up his daughter's decision. "I said, 'Honey, I'm totally with you.'"

He adds:

> The thing is, you need to know what the person needs before the dialogue even starts. You need to know your people. That's what you really need to know. You need to know more about your people. You need to know about what's going on in their lives. You need to know all those things to make them successful so you can become successful.

Take People to a Higher Level

When giving assignments to employees, Richard says he could help them become more effective because he understood what motivated them and what they needed to become successful. When assigning a manager the job of opening an office in another town, he said the manager he chose lived for that kind of challenge. Knowing this woman needed autonomy to get the job done right, he didn't provide her with the steps to proceed because he knew she needed to decide those for herself.

Richard says, contrary to popular belief, money is not the biggest motivator for people. He says this relates to psychologist Abraham Maslow's Hierarchy of Needs, the first of which is self-actualization. Richard says helping people discover and use their inner potential is what makes a boss successful because self-actualization is what every employee needs, whether or not he or she knows it. Employees need to operate at a higher level and be able to make decisions that matter. He explains, "We don't need to tell people how to get things done: We need to tell them what we want done. That's all. And if you have the right people, and you understand what drives them, you can do anything."

With this philosophy, Richard was able to grow the company he led as CEO from a small organization to a multimillion-dollar organization. He gives his people credit for that growth. "I had surrounded myself with brilliant people who I understood. I understood what motivates them." Richard worked hard to get to know his eleven direct reports very well. One part of that was discovering the strengths and weaknesses of his people. Another part was terminating those who were unable to rise to the occasion and complete tasks that he needed to get done. "I was dissatisfied with them and terminated them because they weren't making me successful."

Help People Succeed

Richard says a good business leader takes responsibility for the mistakes of his or her people, and that's what he tried to do with his employees. He says that it was his own failure to better understand his employees who failed that led to their failure. Therefore, he advises all business owners and managers to get to know their people better. When a business owner has a continual problem with an employee, Richard says the business owner should work toward making the problem employee a "best friend."

Sometimes a business owner's first impression of an employee can be wrong. Rather than let that negative perception poison all future interactions with that person, additional mentoring and coaching sessions can help a business owner overcome a bad first impression. Richard explains that if a breakthrough with that employee takes place, then the business owner also succeeds at his or her job because the troubled employee has now become a more valuable asset. This can then become a personal success story for both employer and employee.

Richard says, "It really works. People want to do the best they can do. People want to be successful; they want *you* to be successful."

Top Takeaways

1. Recognize self-interest. Ask people what they need. Open a dialogue with people.

2. Ask questions about people's needs. Listen to customers and make them feel comfortable enough to do business with you again and again.

3. Take people to a higher level. Management master Stephen Covey says we should find our voice and help others find theirs. Everyone likes to join a good mission.

4. Help people succeed. Grow from your mistakes. Take responsibility for your people, taking them under your wing if necessary.

Chapter 10

How to Sell Your Work to Customers

gregarious adj. *socially enjoying companionship with other people*

Thirty years ago, my uncle, Phil Dumont, was a New York City police officer who lived on Long Island with his wife and two sons. After growing up in Brunswick, Maine, and joining the U.S. Army, he spent several years overseas. When he returned to civilian life, he got his dream job as a police officer in New York City. After a couple of squad car accidents that left his back too injured to sit still in a police cruiser or hold up a gun belt, he retired from the job he loved. He then took a job at a nearby startup, Four Seasons Sunrooms, where his wife, Corinne, worked as a bookkeeper. In 1986, after working for the company's founders for several years, he decided to break free and start his own business, Downeast Sun Space, as Four Seasons' first franchise in Maine. The story of his successful business and family offer new business owners many lessons about building skills, starting a business, and recognizing success. A large part of Phil's success is his ability to communicate and work with customers while selling them his products and services.

PHILIP DUMONT, 61—SUNROOM BUILDER FRANCHISEE

Although Phil formally retired from his job as a New York City cop, he basically quit because of painful back injuries that kept him from being able to do the job. Phil's transition from an officer in the NYPD to an independent business owner was the result of many planned and unplanned developments along the way.

While he was still in New York, following his retirement, his wife found a job in the accounting department at Four Seasons, a large sunroom company in Long Island that was pursuing franchising. Phil says, "Then, when they found out I was retired and looking for work, I went in for an interview with the head of corporate. They hired me to run their installation department in Long Island." He figured it would give him something to do.

Suddenly, Phil entered the sunroom industry. He says he learned everything he could. First, he worked with all of the company's installers, learning the trade. Then, he says, he was asked to replace another installer who was moving to another state to open a franchise. The company's decision to begin opening franchises was a turning point for Phil. He recalls, "They started running seminars in the factory for people wanting to open up and start a business."

Live Your Dreams

After living and working in New York for more than a decade, Phil's dreams in life had changed. Now that he was no longer a police officer in New York City, he wanted to get back to his family and friends in Brunswick, Maine, where he grew up. He says:

> I wanted to come back to Maine, and when they went franchising, I was working more inside than outside running seminars on the installation part of the product, teaching the franchisees and their installers how to install. We only had two or three products, so it was relatively simple. As we were getting more people in, I was getting offered jobs to go wherever I wanted to go.

Four Seasons' franchisees from Florida to California wanted Phil to run their installation departments, but he dreamed of moving back to Maine. The idea of opening a franchise in Maine was beginning to grow in his mind. He talked to the company's owner and pitched his idea. The owner also liked the idea. Phil says: "So I decided one day to put my house up for sale. Three days later, the house sold." He was on his way to opening the company's first franchise in Maine.

When Phil first opened his shop, he partnered with a small business owner in Maine who was interested in starting a new venture. In October 1985, they bought the franchise together, which they operated out of Phil's new home in Brunswick. Phil says he sold his first sunroom to the owner of the Maine Mall in his kitchen at the kitchen table. Phil's original plan was for his partner to become a salesperson, "But," Phil says, "nobody cared for him a whole hell of a lot. He got thrown off a couple of jobs."

Phil says the business quickly became too big to run out of his home and he found a building suited to his needs. But conflicts with his partner intensified: "He wanted to build a whole big structure and spend $100,000 on a showroom. Our showroom cost us a hell of a lot less than that." Phil recalls that another reason the partnership crumbled was his partner's inexperience. "He didn't have any construction background, and he wasn't much of a salesman either. He wanted to run his retail rental businesses out of the office."

The relationship with his partner quickly deteriorated. Phil explains, "He stormed out and said, 'I don't want to do this any more.' I said, 'Okay.' We had to buy him out."

After Phil bought out his former partner's share of the business, the sunroom company became a Dumont family business, employing himself, his wife Corinne, and his son Rodney.

Now that his old partner was out, Phil turned his natural affinity for conversation and his love of people into a career in sales that has helped his business and family grow and prosper in the beautiful college town of Brunswick. From the beginning, to ensure he is selling a quality product, he either did the work himself or hired his own workers, including his son Rodney. He never uses subcontractors. He learned that doing the work himself while maintaining his own workforce gave him more control over the kind of work that he wanted to get done. He says, "I would do the work during the day, and I would sell on weekends, and sell at night, to keep it going."

Phil says it took his son, who was eighteen when he started employing him, a short time to get the hang of the job. He adds that, once Rodney conquered his frustrations, he became a top installer who customers requested. "He's an unbelievable installer." After ten years of working side by side, Phil turned the installation side of his business over to his son.

Phil says that it was not an easy decade. "There was a lot of stress trying to be everything for everybody, which is difficult to do. For a couple of years business was slow because of the economy, but most of the time it was good." He adds that his wife's financial skills are vital to the business. "Corinne handles all the money."

Work Your Financial Advantage

Of course, smart financial decisions and a steady cash flow can help any entrepreneur get his or her business off the ground. Part-time jobs, pensions, return on investments, savings, and so forth can help support a business owner until his or her profits from a new business reach comfortably sustainable levels. From the outset, Phil says he had an important source of income that helped him start his own business. "My advantage was I had a police pension. Of course, I put my house up as collateral to buy the building, to renovate it, and get the look that we wanted." The showroom was complete. Every few years since then, he continues to renovate it and upgrade the products he displays there.

Today, open weekdays, Phil's bright Four Seasons showroom displays and demonstrates the latest sunroom products available. The location also serves as the hub where the Dumonts' friends, family members, employees, customers, and pets get together and share their lives while the business hums around them. The atmosphere there is comfortable, warm, and welcoming.

Although many entrepreneurs have difficulty working closely with a spouse, Phil says he has no trouble working with Corinne:

> That was the easiest part, because we've always gotten along. We're best friends. That's why we go on vacation together, and take long car rides together. We'll get up in the morning on a Sunday and go to Canada, and come home. For us, being together all the time, that was the easy part. She made it easy.

Phil says that Corinne's role in the business is essential. She tells him how the company is doing financially, and what needs to be done. Phil also relies on her to tell him when he can spend and when he can't. Corinne handles the money in the office while Phil goes out and handles sales. Their division of work and mutual trust keep their business working smoothly and their employees working.

Today, Phil says his staffing is perfect because of the expertise and quality work of his employees. "Right now, Rodney and [employee] Jeremy, they're like bosom buddies. They know what they're doing. It makes their job easier. Sometimes it might take longer, but I don't care."

Treat Your Employees Like Family

Finding a great employee like Jeremy wasn't easy for Phil. He explains, "I've been through twenty-five workers in the past twenty years." He also says his employees become part of the family. "They're as important to me as my kids are." Phil takes responsibility for his employees' needs by providing them with a solid livelihood. He explains, "That's why Jeremy was able to buy a house and do that kind of stuff." He also makes sure they get vacations when they need time off.

Phil says he enjoys bringing his employees into the family fold, because he has always liked them: "We go to dinner. We have them over to the house."

When subzero temperatures shut down his company's operations during Maine's tough winter months, Phil sometimes needs to lay off his employees so they can collect unemployment. "Unemployment's not bad, and I bring them back as quickly as I can." During the winter months in Maine and other northern regions, most outdoor workers collect unemployment because it's simply too cold to work. Even though Phil has work lined up, bad weather makes it impossible to complete. He says, "You can't put footings in the ground. There are certain things you can't do no matter what."

Jeremy, who is twenty-eight, has been with Downeast Sun Space for five years. Phil says he has long-term plans for his son Rodney as well as his employee Jeremy:

> I want Jeremy to do what Rodney does, and I want Rodney to do what I do, as a gradual release. I'm going to give him

the franchise. I'm going to give it to him, and give him everything that comes along with that: the headaches, the problems. I'm going to sell it to him for a buck.

Phil is still not sure when he'll be ready to turn over his company to his son, because he's not done yet. He knows he'll be ready one day, but first he would like Rodney to take a few management courses. On the other hand, Phil also sees firsthand that his son is becoming an expert in his craft through experience and his mentoring. Phil says, "He knows the product. He knows what it takes to install it, and I think that's what's needed," He also acknowledges that Rodney's expertise in his field helps him work well with customers. "He's good at that. The customers who know him like him."

Be a People Person

Phil sees many of his own positive attributes in his son's gregarious nature and growing people skills. Phil knows customers connect well with him because they frequently invite him to dinner. "I get along well with people. I'm like a 'people person.'"

Phil says that one of his secrets to success is the fact that he enjoys meeting new people:

> I like people, and I care about them. It's not just a sale to me. I go back there all the time to them, even after the job is done. I'll call them up six months later, "How you doin'?" I've got customers in Booth Bay Harbor. Every summer, I call them up, and we go to dinner. Do I have to do that? No, but I like them. There's a guy, I built him a sunroom fifteen years ago; I still call him up to see how he's doing.

When Phil is doing his work, he says, he's not just creating customers, he's making friends. "I think about them a lot." He says his business relationships extend far beyond the sale and installation of a sunroom, "and I think most of them know that."

When he does encounter an occasional difficult customer, Phil doesn't let their tension upset him. He explains: "I get past that. I'm going to be who I am, and Corinne is going to be who she is, and we're going to do what we do."

Phil says he has learned to trust his son Rodney to help make their customers happy. "That's what makes my life easier. Once Rodney gets to the job site, he does what he's going to do, and he's going to please the customer. If the customer isn't pleased, it's because of them, not him."

Assess Your Customers

Part of Phil's business is dealing with people who only want to pick his brain for information but have no intention of buying anything. Phil says these types of customers don't bother him. He gives them a quote, doing the same amount of work he would do for anyone else. He says, "I don't treat them any differently, but I can pretty well tell I'm wasting my time. But it just gives me a little bit more enthusiasm for the next one. People are going to be what they are. I'm not going to fault them for it. I'm just going to do what I do."

Another kind of customer is the person who really can't afford the product or service he or she is seeking. Phil says he tells these people that they are not ready for his product. Instead of trying to sell a customer a product that is inappropriate for the situation, he instead tells the person the hard truth. "You really shouldn't do this. You've got windows you've got to replace. You need to allocate your dollars elsewhere to make your life better. And if you want a sunroom down the road, terrific."

Customers have specific needs, and often they don't truly understand what those needs are. Great salespeople use their keenest insights to review a customer's situation and real needs. Look around. Ask many questions. The bottom line is not always the sale. With a sharp eye on a person's needs, you can better assess what you can offer that person. If your product or service is inappropriate for the situation, truthfulness and support can build relationships for the future, when your product or service is more appropriate. Plus, future sales can be even more fruitful than a quick but inappropriate sale. Observing, listening, learning, and nurturing are keys to your customers' needs. It took Phil a few years to learn this. He says, "Over a period of time you realize that sometimes people don't know what they want for themselves."

Pick Your Prize

An entrepreneur also needs to decide whether he or she wants to cope with the challenges of larger commercial jobs, or to stick with a broader base of individual, residential sales. Although he once did them, Phil is not interested in large commercial jobs anymore. Although many entrepreneurs dream of contracting large jobs with big businesses, Phil prefers to work with individual customers. He likes working with homeowners. "They're better to deal with. I find it more satisfying dealing with them."

Do Marketing and Advertising

Whereas James Mervine's (see Chapter 5) only marketing is a business card that he updates with a pen before handing it to potential clients, Phil gets most of his customers by advertising in the local newspaper. Although he also gets leads from his corporate headquarters, most of them don't pan out, even after he has sent the potential customer a brochure and cover letter. Advertising works for his type of product, but some forms of media are more effective than others.

Phil says, "We did one TV ad. We got a job from that, but that actually broke out even." The sale of the sunroom only brought in enough to cover the cost of the advertisement, so Phil no longer advertises on television.

Now, he runs newspaper ads throughout most of the year, except in the dead of winter. At the end of March he'll start running the ads in three or four of the region's newspapers. The results are completely unpredictable. He says: "It's funny. Certain years, certain areas will sell, and others don't. And other years, different areas will sell, and others don't. You don't know."

Determine How You Want to Grow

Two full-time employees besides himself and his wife is a perfect size for his operation, Phil says. "I'm not going to get bigger," he adds. Phil lets his customers know up front how long he expects it will take to complete a job with his small workforce and Maine's dynamic weather, but he says most of them forget and need reminding of the realities of the job. Although he always rushes to fix emergencies, he also will not tolerate being harassed by a needy customer who puts undue pressure on him or his workers to complete a job faster. Quality work takes time, and Phil won't risk quality to rush a job. He is also willing to drop customers who give him a hard time. He says, "I would rather not do the work and lose the sale than get somebody jumping on me to hurry up and get there."

Staying on a job until it is done right is the way Phil takes care of his customers. He explains, "I'm here to go long term. I'm not here to try to get as many sales as I can and then get out."

Phil tells his employees to take their time to satisfy the customer. "If it takes longer, so what? I don't care." He'd rather have employees take a week longer to finish a job and get it right than have them hurry and have to go back again and again to fix problems from shoddy workmanship. Plus, his customers are his neighbors and friends, so he cares deeply about maintaining his reputation for quality work.

It took twelve years of self-employment before Phil was really content as a business owner, but he feels like he put most of the pressure on himself:

> When you open up a franchise, and they're telling you that "it's a multimillion dollar franchise and you're going to do really well, and you're going to make money as long as you listen to what we tell you," it's all crap. It's not true. You only make it if you care about people and you care about your product, and you're not just there to sell it.

Make Smart Decisions

Phil says starting his own business was the best decision he has ever made because it gives him more time with the people he loves. "It affords me the ability to give for my family more than I ever would have done in any other way." Now that he no longer builds the sunrooms himself, he is more available to help his large family in dozens of ways. He says, "I get to relate to my family a lot more. I help everybody."

The flexibility of self-employment allows Phil to spend more time with his parents, children, grandchildren, brothers, sisters, and friends. Most of them live in Brunswick or nearby. "Living is easier. It was a good decision." He says that decision is one of the reasons his family has done so well. Making the decision was not easy, he explains, and he often misses his old job as a police officer in New York City.

As many self-employed people have discovered, serendipity plays a strange role in entrepreneurship. Being able to take advantage of the opportunities it brings is what makes a business succeed. Phil credits his wife and the company where she worked with his opportunity to start a business, but he says he never planned to be where he is today, making a living selling and installing sunrooms for his own company.

> We always thought she'd be working for somebody, and I was going to be a policeman for twenty-five years, retire, and maybe come back to Maine, maybe not. The kids would be out. But, the way that it turned out, it gave everybody the opportunity to come back [to Maine], open up a franchise, have a business, and turn it over to someone who didn't know what he was going to do in his life.

Phil's plan for his life as a police officer changed after his back injuries. He didn't want to retire. He didn't want to leave the job he loved, but the injuries changed the direction of his career. Phil then turned his experience and skills as a "people person" into a better way of life for himself and his family through a self-employment opportunity that emerged from the place he worked.

Trust Your People

Trust is also the essence of Phil's relationships with his employees, including his son. Some entrepreneurs burden themselves with so many worries during the day that they have difficulty turning off the business side of their brains at night. Phil has learned from years of experience how to sleep soundly without business worries because he knows his people have done their best work. He explains:

> I realized I can't please everybody, and Rodney does the best he can. And he's there to please me, which took me a while to realize that. It took him a while to be there as well. Because he knows that it is as important to him as it is to me, because if he's going to do what I do, he doesn't want to fail. He doesn't want to take a business that's been in

business for twenty-five years and have it fail on his watch. So, I don't worry about him doing the work, and I don't worry about customers much because I can usually sit and talk with them and accommodate their issues 99 percent of the time.

As a manager, Phil sees himself as a buffer between his front-line people and the customers. This helps jobs move forward without getting his people wrapped up in customers' personal problems.

When selling his products and services, Phil sometimes has to turn down installation and repair work that involves too much liability for his business. He has learned from experience which jobs to avoid, because fixing other workers' shoddy work can be like opening a can of worms. He says: "I've been called on other jobs that other sunroom people have done, who want me to go out and fix it, and I tell them, "I can't do it, because if I touch it, I own it, and every problem you're ever going to have forever belongs to me. You didn't buy it from me, so I can't. I feel bad, I'm sorry, but . . . "

He adds, "I'm conscientious about all the work we do. You've got to do it from start to finish."

Take Care of Customers While Selling to Make a Profit

Phil's strategy for taking care of his customers' needs is fairly simple: be honest with them, and don't sell yourself short. He says:

Don't sell the job just to get it, because if you do, you're going to end up getting the short end of the stick. Sell it to make a profit. I tell them, "Listen, if I can't sell it and make a profit, I won't be here next year. Who are you going to have to make any repairs for any damages that may or may not happen to your roof?" You've got to be up front with people. You can't let them bully you into telling you that they can get it cheaper somewhere else.

He adds, "Whatever business you go into, you've got to make sure you know it, because it's going to take a lot of hours at the beginning of it to get it off the ground. But be tenacious." Doing the hard work at the beginning of a business to get started is the most important step of all.

When he was working at the Four Seasons headquarters, Phil took advantage of on-the-job training opportunities so he could learn the business, which helped him become self-employed. He also benefited from Corinne's experience in the company's accounting department: She could handle the books of a franchise. They both gained their skills by working side by side with the corporate parent's best people. Once they gained the skills to run a business, Phil says selling the product is easy. "Selling it is just selling. You put numbers together and sell the product without lying to your customer. You've got to just listen to your customers, and not convince them to do something they do not want to do. Just listen to them."

Phil says he does not believe in using intrusive sales methods, such as cold calling and door-to-door solicitation, to sell his product. He simply places advertisements in local newspapers and lets customers come to him. He has never tried to sell something to people who haven't inquired first.

"Make Some Money and Enjoy It"

When offering advice to would-be entrepreneurs, Phil says, "The biggest thing is you've got to be willing to put in the time to make it work." When he first started, he says, he worked six long days a week installing and selling sunrooms. "I did it because I wanted to succeed—that's the Dumont thing—and I enjoyed doing the work. I enjoyed being a cop more, because that was a service industry." Because he can no longer do the work of a police officer, he instead enjoys working with customers to get them the quality services and products they want. "This is satisfying because when you get finished with a product that's done, customers have spent their money, and they're going to enjoy it forever. That's the kind of thing I like."

Phil credits his wife Corinne with keeping him motivated through any tough times. From the start, their business made a good profit. "We were successful early on, so we were able to get off the deck fairly quickly."

Today, Phil's main goal as a salesperson is to keep his crew working. He explains that business basically comes down to three things, "We want something to do, make some money, and enjoy it."

After his first few years, Phil's success gave him the confidence to experiment with growth. He expanded his business by opening a second franchise in another part of the state. He says the logistics and staffing issues of running two separate operations were not worth the headaches. After two years, he closed his second franchise to concentrate on his first business. He recalls, "It was taking too much time. You multiplied the work, but you didn't multiply the dollars you earned."

Paying bills on time over the long haul is how business owners develop credit and better terms with banks and suppliers. It also helps them keep employees. A new business owner needs good credit to get a company to run. Building trust with suppliers takes time. Corinne is good at it, so Phil says he never worries about it: "She makes sure all our bills are paid. Employees get paid first." He explains: "There was a time when it was real slow. I wouldn't get paid for six or seven months, but it didn't matter as long as they got paid and we had money coming in, and we were paying the bills, and paying insurances and advertising."

Although Phil has considered retirement in the past, he says he's having too much fun working for himself to stop any time soon. He likes meeting new customers and sometimes takes friends and family members with him when he makes sales calls. They keep him company while he drives long distances around the region taking care of business. By including family in his business and running it with his wife and son, Phil finds himself enjoying the most satisfying experience of his life.

Maintain Your Equipment

One strategy for saving money over the long term is buying new vehicles. With regular service, property, equipment, and vehicles help business owners earn money instead of spending it on costly repairs. Phil buys new vehicles and invests around $2,000 per year to keep them serviced. He says, "Get the oil changed, maintain them, drive them easily. The oil change and servicing is everything."

Wisely Consider Partners

After a negative experience with his initial business partner, Phil believes that business owners are better off without partners. "Do it on your own. If you make it, you make it; if you fail, you fail." When he bought out his partner, Phil became a sole proprietor. He says, "The business became ultimately easier."

Starting with a partner was the one mistake Phil says he made when he opened his business. "I realized I didn't need him. It didn't take him long to realize, no, this is not for me." After a year in business, he invested more money into his business and became partner-free.

The first year of his business was the most difficult. Neither of his children wanted to leave New York, and his wife missed her friends there. Today, all of them are happy they made the move. He says: "I personally think it was the best move we made. And it gave us the opportunity to be successful, and be able to help them." Now, twenty-five years later, evidence of the Dumont's close family ties is all over town: As adults, both of Phil and Corinne's sons, Rodney and Randy—and their growing families—have chosen to live in Brunswick near their parents. In addition, Phil and his brothers, Michael and Ronald, continue to live near their own parents with their families as well. Ronald stops by Phil and Corinne's office several times a week, sometimes with their father, Joe. Other days, Ronald joins Phil on sales calls, just to spend time with his younger brother.

A successful family is one sure sign of business success.

Top Takeaways

1. Live your dreams. Keep your eyes on the prize. If you have a destination in mind, share it with others and stay focused on reaching it over the long term.

2. Work your financial advantage. If you have built up a financial nest egg with savings, a pension, an insurance payoff, an inheritance, or any other lump sum that can help you start a business, make the most of it by using it wisely to attain your vision.

3. Treat your employees like family. Because it is so hard to find good people, once you find them, treat them like you would want to be treated so they stick around.

4. Be a people person. Sales require a certain savvy with people. If you have it, work it. If you aren't good with people, find somebody who is better with them to do your selling.

5. Assess your customers. Not every customer is one you should keep. If you are making low returns on time-consuming individuals, don't waste your time and effort trying to satisfy them. Some people just want to bend your ear.

6. Pick your prize. Find your niche and stick with it. Do only the jobs that make you happy. Working with bad customers can drastically lower your job satisfaction.

7. Do marketing and advertising. Although some entrepreneurs don't need advertising or marketing thanks to their solid connections in the marketplace, it is worth trying a few affordable avenues of marketing and advertising to see what might work for you.

8. Determine how you want to grow. As Bo Burlingham points out in his book *Small Giants*, bigger is not always better. If your business is a comfortable size, don't knock yourself out trying to make it bigger. Keep your job satisfaction at the forefront of your decisions.

9. Make smart decisions. Sound judgment is the hallmark of a great leader. Consider your choices, do your research, prepare wisely, and take action.

10. Trust your people. Relationships are built on trust, and you have to give it to get it. When employees prove themselves worthy of your trust, give them more.

11. Take care of customers while selling to make a profit. Be honest with people. Customers expect you to keep your bottom line in mind when making business decisions.

12. "Make some money and enjoy it." Work hard, but don't kill yourself. Today's efforts will pay off tomorrow. If you are unhappy doing what you do, do something else.

13. Maintain your equipment. Taking care of your investments saves you time and money in the long run.

14. Wisely consider partners. Look at all of the long-term ramifications of a partner before signing the bottom line.

Chapter 11

How to Grow

success n. **1** *a positive outcome* **2** *a person who succeeds*

In terms of dollars, property, friends, family, cars, vehicles, and so forth, one of the most successful of my close friends from high school is Joseph P. Kelly. I met him during the summer while I was working as a disc jockey at my high school radio station. He was passing by the window and looked in because he heard loud music playing. He soon joined the station and became Joey Komatose, a popular rock-and-roll DJ at WMPH-FM.

After graduating from Mount Pleasant High School in 1986, Joe joined the Air Force instead of going to college. Now, more than twenty years later, he has done quite well for himself as a small-business owner. Actually, the term *small business* barely applies to him these days, now that he has approximately fifty employees and a fleet of many types of service vehicles. His equipment overshadows the lonely pressure washer on a trailer with which he started his business only a decade ago. His rapid growth and stellar success are the results of nothing less than hard work, diligence, a talent for working with people, and the management skills he learned from his own experiences in a variety of leadership roles over the years.

JOSEPH P. KELLY JR., 40—COMMERCIAL CONTRACTOR

After another long day of keeping track of his growing business, Joe points out that he has recently changed his business hours. "Last year was the first year I stopped working Saturdays."

Joe started Kelly's Hot Pressure Washing back in 1995 in Wilmington, Delaware, while he was a full-time employee of a large regional grocery chain with more than 135 supermarkets under its banner. He says:

> I was working part time at night with my neighbor who was a heating and air conditioner technician. He did it on the side. He was in the National Guard, and I was his, what they call "tin knocker," where you put all the ductwork together. He paid me $12 an hour to do really, really [manual labor]. I mean, the amount of money that I got paid and the amount of money that he got paid for me doing what I did was ridiculous.

Joe did the hard work of a tin knocker because he needed extra money to help support his wife and two young children. He was already working in a grocery store forty-eight hours a week, but it wasn't enough, so he got a side job. He says, "I worked three four-to six-hour nights during the week doing the ductwork building. I did that for about a year, earning money."

When he first got out of the service, he went back to work for the union he left to join the Air Force. He became the grocery store's nighttime baker. Joe says, "With the benefits that I had in the union, I was making the top rate, because when you leave for the service, your seniority increases as if you were still working there. I was making $8 an hour when I left, so when I got out, I was making $12.50, which was the top union rate." Even with the extra fifty cents per hour he was making working on the night crew, and the time-and-a-half pay he was getting working eight hours of overtime each week, Joe was unsatisfied.

As an ambitious young worker, he jumped at every chance he could to earn more money. He worked every holiday for time and a half. He moved from department manager to bakery manager, which freed up his evenings to do HVAC work with his friend at night. This helped him meet all of the expenses of his growing family, but he still wanted something different. He began to think about self-employment as a better option. He says, "As that was going on, I was looking for something that I could do myself, because I felt smarter than Mike, and *I* was doing the idiot work."

Meanwhile, unknown to him at the time, the first half of the biggest opportunity in his career was waiting in his father's backyard. He recalls:

> My dad and brother were cleaning their deck. My dad took a whole week's vacation to clean his deck, and they were doing it with a scrub brush and some kind of cleaner. So I did some research on how to clean decks. The deal was that you were supposed to use a pressure washer with cold water, but at the time hot water pressure washing was the new latest and greatest technology. It was a diesel or kerosene fired burner that generated heat to facilitate the hot water for the pressure washing, which made your cleaning time half. I was all about efficiency.

While researching pressure washers, a strange coincidence happened. Around this same time, Joe started earning some extra money from his uncle who owned a pallet company. Joe learned to rebuild pallets, and they paid him $1 per pallet. In the industrial zone where he rebuilt pallets, Joe found the second crucial half of the equation that would transform him into his own full-time boss. He recalls, "Where the pallet plant was, there was a mechanic who was going through a divorce who had a hot pressure washer that he needed to unload for $1,500 because he wanted to liquidate all of his stuff before they went through the divorce."

Joe says he put two and two together. He says:

> I made my dad a deal that if he would buy me the pressure washer I would pressure wash his deck for the rest of his life, and that I would pay him back the $1,500 I borrowed from him. So I practiced on some friends' decks and put out an ad in the local newspaper. I got some jobs.

Work Hard to Make It Work

Joe bought the pressure washer and starting cleaning friends' decks at half price to learn his new trade. Suddenly, he had a part-time business on the side of his full-time job as a grocery store manager.

To determine the right price to charge for his services, Joe did some research. He says, "I went to the contractors association and figured out what the going rate was for pressure washing doing commercial and government jobs. That number is nationally produced, so I figured that out." He also called other pressure-washing companies and asked them for their rates. Although most contractors don't want to give prices over the phone, Joe used his negotiation skills to get some estimates. He also learned by trial and error. He explains: "The first couple of jobs you've got to figure out square footage, so you give a couple estimates and you don't get the job because you're too high." Finding the right price can be difficult. When he got it wrong, Joe says he took it personally: "When you go out to your first job with your pressure washer, and you've got all your stuff together, and you think you're a pressure-washing contractor, and you give somebody a price that's too high, it's emotional that you lost the job."

One book about building a business that helped Joe get started was *Think and Grow Rich* by Napoleon Hill. Joe read it when he was twenty years old, but he says the lessons stuck with him:

> The whole deal is you have to make calculated risks to succeed. That was his whole premise. Say, everybody is working in the blue-collar deal: well, how did you become a white-collar guy? Well, you've got to jump ship. I learned that when I was in the union and when I was in the service.

In the Air Force, Joe learned that there were always two types of people: those who want to grow and succeed, and those who just want to get by with the minimal amount of work. He says, "These are just average guys, so if I just do a little bit more than them, I'm going to succeed." He decided he wanted to take advantage of the opportunities available in the service and elsewhere.

Joe says that's when he learned to compete to win:

> So, if you're a one-striper and they say, "In three months we're going to do a class for Senior Airman Below-the-Zone [BTZ, a competitive Air Force leadership training process] which is so that when you get two stripes, you can get your third stripe six months early if you can go through this exam. Basically, you go in front of your commander in your blues and you have to know current events and Air Force history, and Air Force knowledge, and all that stuff, but also your buttons and pins and medals all have to be straight, and you have to have a good haircut.

Joe stepped up to the challenge because he knew that he could perform better than his peers. He also wanted the early raises and extra money received by high achievers in the Air Force. The system helped him excel. He says, "If you start putting a little effort into that, then, all of a sudden, you're not in the average group just getting by."

In the service, when you step up to a challenging promotion and succeed, you need to keep working hard to impress your superiors. When he became a Senior Airman BTZ, his superiors suddenly had higher expectations for his performance. Joe says, "You almost want to create expectations to live by so that you have to live up to those expectations every day, or else people are going to think that even though you are above average, they're going to think you're a failure if you can't keep the above-average momentum going."

Set High Expectations

While Joe was in the service, he set high expectations for himself. Then he went to the academy for noncommissioned officers (NCO), where he received a star to go with his stripes on his uniform. Through his extra effort, Joe got recognized for his achievements. He says:

> I'm already six months ahead of everybody, and I go to this thing, and there's a leadership award. It's the same deal. You have to go to this class. You have no choice. You can't

say, "I'm a Sergeant and I don't want to go to this class." It's a military thing. You have to do it.

Once again, Joe increased his effort and became a contender for two of the Air Force's highest honors. One of the awards is for the highest score on a grueling test. The other award is the John Levitow Award for the first NCO to show extraordinary leadership. John Levitow was loadmaster for an AC-47 gunship whose heroism during wartime made him the lowest-ranking airman to ever be awarded the Medal of Honor by the Air Force. On February 24, 1969, during the height of the Vietnam War, he performed a bloody act of bravery and self-sacrifice over North Vietnam, saving an aircraft's pilot and eight-man crew.

While attending the NCO Academy, Joe set himself apart from his peers by winning the John Levitow Award as the result of his performance as a leader during leadership training sessions. He explains, "Somebody has to step up."

Look for Opportunities to Learn

After leaving the Air Force, Joe returned to his union job at the grocery store. He says the situation at the store was similar to his experiences in the Air Force: Some people step up, others don't. Some workers were simply waiting for an across-the-board raise. Others tried to stand out from their peers by taking their leadership roles seriously. Joe says:

> I was looking for an opportunity to make more money and excel with opportunities. That's what happened with the contracting thing. It was like, do I want to be some dude knocking tin, or do I want to be the guy telling the guy to knock the tin? Well, I wanted to be the guy that is not the guy who's knocking the tin. It just happened that the pressure washing thing just all worked out.

Joe's self-employment adventure started when he decided to solve his father's deck-cleaning problem. "My dad is struggling on his deck for three days, and I know there is an easier way to do it. So, I figured out the easier way." That's when Joe had his career-changing serendipitous moment:

Just coincidentally, where I'm moonlighting in the palette business, there's a mechanic who's getting a divorce that's got to get rid of this pressure washer that's the solution for my dad's deck. I knew that the solution to his deck was a pressure washer, and just in that sequence of time, I'm looking for something to do on my own part time that is something that I can do, that is relatively easy in the contracting field.

Joe saw the potential to transform the divorcing man's pressure washer into a contracting profession. Knocking tin helped him decide that he wanted to find an opportunity to do something people needed. The pressure washer was his key to solving customers' problems.

Joe explains that he grows his company by doing high-quality work to earn repeat business: "The pressure-washing business is all repeat business. It's all word of mouth. I put an ad in the paper, but there's another key phrase: the acquisition and maintenance of customers." Joe explains that once he's done the hard work of acquiring a customer, that customer should be thought of as permanent. He says: "He's paid you, and now you've acquired him. Now, the easy part is to maintain him." By keeping all of his customers happy by following up and ensuring repeat business, he grows his business by continually adding new, long-term customers to his client list and maintaining his accounts. After a couple of years of this, when Joe got to the point where he could no longer serve all of his customers by himself, he says, "I had to hire somebody."

Working many hours, Joe follows this smart equation and grows his business. His first year as a contractor was hectic because he was also working overtime at the grocery store. He says:

In my pressure-washing world, I had to open up the store at 6 A.M., and I was off at 2:30 or 3 P.M., and then I scheduled my first pressure washing job at 5 P.M., so I had a half an hour to get home, half an hour to get something to eat, kiss the baby, load my truck up, put my rig on the back, and off I went. I had a job set up four days a week. And when I wasn't doing a job, I was bidding a job.

At the time, Joe continued to move up in his full-time union job as well. He was given the difficult assignment of helping to turn around one of the worst stores in the large chain. One reason why the store was doing so poorly was because it was in a rough neighborhood in Woodland, Pennsylvania. Joe says, "It's a grocery store in the ghetto, so there were shoplifters. I worked there, and I did that, and I did pretty well at it." Joe did so well that the company asked him to leave the union to become a company manager. The grocery store chain paid to send him to management school. He spent the next six months putting on a suit and driving an hour to Malvern, Pennsylvania to learn the finer points of leadership and grocery store management.

Meanwhile, his business was growing like crazy on the side. He would take breaks to go into the bathroom where he used his cell phone to take calls and book jobs. He explains, "I've got two guys working for me now. I'm making more with my side work than I am with my regular job, but I've got to keep my regular job because I've got a family, and contracting is not a stable deal."

Another pressure he faced at this time was a family who had always worked for other people. He explains:

> Anyone in my family never took a risk to get a reward like that. My old man worked for the same company for thirty-five years. And his dad did, and all that, so when I stopped and left [the company] and moved three states away to be on my own, everyone thought I was out of my mind.

Watch Your Bottom Line

While living in Delaware, Joe continued to juggle work, family, and more training. Even after his management training ended and he was anointed a manager, his company sent him to more leadership training classes around the world.

Joe suddenly found himself earning a manager's salary in a rough location. He says: "They put me in the worst store in Delaware on Dupont Street. The store hadn't made money in ten years."

As an incentive to turn the store around, Joe says his district manager challenged him by offering him a large bonus. Joe says he took the challenge:

I'm chasing shoplifters because they're taking money off my bottom line that's going to get me my bonus. I chased a guy up a fire escape for a steak! I'm telling you, I chased a dude for a watermelon, and took the knee out of my suit! I'm chasing him, and tackled him in the parking lot, for like $5 because it's coming off my bottom line!

Joe was determined to get his bonus money. One day, a local drug addict decided to rob the grocery store. Joe tells the story:

He came in and stole hair color, and two hours later he came in—he had blonde hair, and he comes in with black hair—and thinks he's going to rob the place. He's got a bag. He's so lit up! I'm watching him, and he thinks he's going to make a break for it, and I just go up and grab him. He's all strung out. He has no idea what's going on. So, I restrain him, take our merchandise, call the law. The law comes and they ask, "Do you want to press charges?"

I'm like, "No, I'm just after my merchandise."

The cop said, "Man, there's something wrong with you!"

I said, "This is coming off my bottom line!"

Joe's vigilance put an end to much of the shoplifting that previously plagued the store. He says, "They thought I was crazy because I was over the top with shoplifting and theft and all that."

Stop Putting Money into Somebody Else's Pocket

Joe's unorthodox management strategies proved to be effective. His store's positive sales numbers showed that he had reached the financial goal he needed to receive his hefty bonus. He says when he asked his district management about the money, his boss told him the bonus was much less than he expected.

Joe says he was enraged. "This guy didn't pay me my bonus, and I threatened him, and told him that I didn't care where he got it from, but I was coming to his house after work and I'm going to get my money."

Once Joe calmed down from the initial shock of not getting the money he worked so hard to earn, he realized he had many things to consider at this point in his career. On one hand, he already had two employees and two trucks working for his growing pressure-washing business. On the other hand, he had a well-paying management position at a company that had been very good to him, his father, and his whole family for many, many years. He says he regretted making the threat, because he should have been thinking about and showing respect for his family instead.

Although he had calmed down, he was still furious. The next day, when he went to work, his boss told him he was insubordinate. He wasn't getting fired, but he needed to forget about the bonus he had been promised. It still wasn't happening. Joe says:

> My district manager who threw that lofty bonus out at me hid behind the vice president. He brought him with him. I said, "Let's put it all out on the table. If we're telling the truth, let's tell the truth."
>
> And I said, "Jim, what did you tell me about my bonus? Right. And you can only pay me a portion of it? I'm here busting my balls at 3 in the morning doing inventory and all this stuff to make money, and you won't pay me?"

Suddenly, Joe says his future became clear: He needed to quit. He explains, "That's when I realized that the more effort you put into somebody else's pocket, the less that you make for yourself." Doing the math, he realized that his growing business could soon earn him as much money as he was making on his manager's salary if he did it full time. If he started earning more customers now, in a few years he would have a solid customer base to support his family without the stress of having a boss who won't pay a promised bonus. Joe explains:

> If you're working for the man, if you're busting your butt and you're working for somebody else, a corporate company, you're not retaining that. If you're on a salary making $35,000 a year, and you're putting in seventy hours to make this bonus, and then they don't pay you! But if you put seventy hours into your own business, you're going to get paid. And it might not be that day, that week, that month, that year, but moving forward . . .

Question People Inside the Industry

With his hot pressure-washing business booming and his day job becoming less important, Joe, the full-time grocery store manager, was poised to become a full-time contractor. Before he quit, he drove to North Carolina to meet the potential customers he needed to seal the deal.

Joe found success in North Carolina because he had a friend who had recently moved to the region. His high school friend, general contractor Paul Houghton, played a crucial role in the early days of his company in North Carolina. Paul moved there from Delaware while Joe was in the service and started his own carpentry business in which he did interior finishing on new homes. Joe visited Paul in North Carolina while he was there to take his children to the North Carolina state fair where they could learn to milk cows. He says, "I had four weeks vacation from the union, and I'm visiting my buddy."

In North Carolina, Joe sought out contracting opportunities. He says he drove by one job site where he saw people doing shoddy pressure washing, and he knew he could do better. After two years in the trade, he asked the right questions to find out the going rates for pressure washers in North Carolina. That's when he met an on-site production manager who answered his questions about prices and job availability. Joe recalls:

> Well, they were building 600 houses. This guy's got the contract for all 600 houses, and he's getting paid $150 a house on a contract, where you don't have to talk to a homeowner. You don't have to go back to the homeowner and collect a check. It's contractor work, so you sign the contract with the company. You send them an invoice; they send you payment.

Joe liked the sound of this kind of commercial arrangement, and decided to pursue it. Switching his business model from residential to commercial allowed him to eliminate the complex and sometimes frustrating work of dealing with individual residential customers from his selling and collections equation. Joe says, "This was very appealing to me."

Three months later, Joe drove back to North Carolina from Delaware to attend the Rockingham NASCAR race, where Paul introduced him to several large southern builders. He connected with them and started to build the network that would help him succeed. Joe recalls:

> It was the first time I ever met them. They all knew Paul. They were all drinking and carrying on. I can't even understand what they're saying because they're Southern. I'm just trying to be the cool guy and make some relationships.

At the NASCAR race, he met a builder who told him about a large privately owned company from Atlanta that was about to start building hundreds of homes in North Carolina. Joe jumped at the opportunity:

> This was like 1999. The building industry wasn't even banging back then. Now, the building industry is carrying the national economy. This was like foresight. This kid was saying to me, "You've got to go get some work with Colony Homes." So I find out who the guy at Colony Homes is. I come down here, and stay at Pauly's, and I have two business meetings with this guy, and sign a contract.

Joe signed the contract while he was still working as a grocery store manager full time in Delaware.

Joe says it was a difficult balancing act "I'm living on the edge here. This guy is going to pay me $150 [each]. He's going to build 600 homes." That was more than Joe made in two years at the grocery store. He commuted to North Carolina several times over the next few months to do work he acquired there.

When he suddenly didn't get the bonus he expected, Joe decided to quit his job and start his own full-time business.

Take Calculated Risks

Before he quit, Joe waited two weeks and got more contracts established in North Carolina. Then he gave his boss his two weeks notice. Next, he went to North Carolina, rented a house, went back to Delaware, packed up his family, and moved. It was in the summertime, so he enrolled his children in local schools so they could start school in North Carolina at the beginning of September.

Joe says his family was concerned about his decision to quit his job:

> Everybody thought I was nuts. I was the first one to leave, and the first one to take a calculated risk. I'm renting a house for $1,200, and I've got a mortgage in New Castle for six months, so I'm juggling two households, which sucked.

While he worked, he was fielding calls from his Realtor. He left his house at 6 A.M. and returned home after dark. Lights on his rig helped him work after dark. He did whatever dirty job he could find. He recalls, "I'm cleaning brick on commercial buildings. I cleaned streets."

Joe says he got into the street-sweeping business by chance, too. One day, a contractor asked him if he could clean streets. Joe told him he could, and went to the store and bought a fire hose. With his wife, Michelle, at the fire hydrant and Joe at the other end, he cleaned a subdivision with a fire hose for $250.

Today, after eight years of steady growth, Joe has improved his street-cleaning process with state-of-the-art equipment. He says, "Right now, I'm cleaning 35 subdivisions with a $110,000 street-cleaning truck with a guy driving it."

Joe says his current success is a result of his willingness to take calculated risks. "If you're willing to take the risk, you've just got to work. I probably worked between sixty- and seventy-hour a week."

Create More Ways to Make Money

Hiring more workers for his business was his next big task. The additional labor was an entirely new challenge. Joe drove his crew to job sites and worked with them during his first year. He explains:

> And then I got another truck here, and then I had two crews going where I was a driver and I had another guy driving. And we worked, worked, worked. Then I got some other opportunities with the street cleaning, so we pressure washed four days, and street cleaned.

Once his business began to grow with more employees and equipment, Joe's company, now called Kelly's Hot Pressure Washing, became a competitor in the local contracting field. He was competing with companies that had much better equipment, which seemed far out of reach for him. He explains, "That was a fantasy. I mean, how in the world could you ever spend $60,000 and go into that much debt on a truck?"

Without extra money to spend on expensive equipment, Joe improvised a low-cost solution. He took a giant, five-foot-diameter reel that was once used for putting in underground wire and attached it to a stand on the back of his truck. The big reel was used to coil and uncoil 300 feet of hose that was attached to a water meter. Joe explains, "We'd have a guy in the back with the big reel and a pair of gloves on, and we'd just roll the reel on this rig I made up by hand. We got a bunch of work from it." The customized truck allowed him to create a street cleaning crew that worked on Fridays and Saturdays.

Using secondhand and modified vehicles or equipment is a competitive investment strategy that saves startup costs for many entrepreneurs. Joe says it has helped him lower his risks. "The one thing I never did, until I acquired the business, I never invested in my acquisition. Until I had the contract signed, I didn't make the investment anticipating it. And then I made the investment after a certain period of having my contract."

Focus on Priorities

When Joe felt limited by the amount of time in the day the sun allowed him to clean streets, he fought back with another contraption. He rigged up lights on his vehicles so he could work at night. He thought, "Darkness isn't going to mess with me. I'm going to buy some lights."

Working seven days a week put tension on his family life, making his first year of business very difficult on everyone. His daughter was in second grade. His son was in kindergarten. He recognized that he was missing out on important time in the lives of his family members. He explains:

> I told my wife, "I'll put my head down for a year. We'll look back and it's not going to be so bad. This is the sacrifice that

I need to make to keep you here to take care of these kids." It was a mutual agreement that "I would rather work two jobs, and you raise my children. That's the way that I want to do it, and if that's our agreement, if you're willing to do it, I'm willing to work two jobs to get us enough income to do that."

Joe tries to keep his business and family in perspective. He explains, "You can't be out working like an idiot if your family's going to pot, because you're really working for your family."

After nearly a decade of building his business into a success, he says his family continues to keep him grounded: "If I didn't have a family and I had what I have now, I'd be dead. I would be dead! I'm telling you. I'm glad I have a family."

Work Harder Than Everyone Else

From the start, Joe has worked hard every day to make his business and family a success. The first year was the most difficult because his work was so demanding. The only day he took off that year was Christmas. He even worked half a day on Thanksgiving. He says, "I had to work because I made that calculated risk to move here, and I wasn't going to be a failure doing it. So I did what I had to do."

Over the following year, Joe saw another contracting opportunity, which soon became his second company: Kelly's Erosion Control. While pressure washing a house one day, the builder was complaining because he couldn't get a certificate of occupancy. Joe recalls:

He's [upset] because he needed a silt fence, which is a fabric attached to stakes to separate his house that's closed from a house that's under construction. The city wouldn't give him this permit unless he had the silt fence up. So I said, "What's the big deal with the silt fence?"

He said, "You've got to dig a trench and hammer the stakes in the ground, and back-fill the fence."

All of the supplies Joe needed were available at Home Depot. Calculating the price of the job against the cost of labor and materials, he saw the potential for a profitable business. He says, "The next week I had a silt fence business and a pressure-washing business."

Looking back on his many business opportunities that have panned out, Joe admits that sometimes he was just lucky. He says, "I got a couple of breaks."

In two years, Joe turned his part-time operation with a single pressure washer into a full-time job involving a fleet of vehicles and a staff of workers performing pressure washing, erosion control, and street cleaning. Today, his companies bring in more money than he ever imagined. Joe says he measures his success by the height of his pile of invoices each week. Judging by the height of his outgoing weekly invoices, Joe's businesses are doing very well. "Now, every week, I probably produce about three to six inches of invoices. It's crazy. I have so much income coming in now, it's stupid," he laughs. "It's ridiculous!"

Grow Naturally with Loyal Customers

Joe's revenues have increased every year he's been in operation by 15 to 20 percent. The structure of his business includes a strategy of having contracts in place before buying new equipment. Instead of buying a brand new, state-of-the-art shop, he bought an old shop and improved it with renovations. As his business grows, he adds more equipment and tools to the shop. Working first and buying later creates substantial savings. Joe explains, "Since we've been in business for ten years, now we're actually lowering our fixed costs and increasing our revenue by just keeping a steady amount of volume."

Joe says his primary focus today is taking care of his customers. By keeping business at a steady level, natural growth comes with loyal customers. He explains:

> As we're servicing people, our customers are growing as well, because everyone wants to grow their business. So, if you can grow together with your customer, and if they're loyal to you, and you can get their loyalty and trust, you've got to screw up to lose your increase in revenue. If you have something go wrong on your job and you're not all over it,

and fix it to make everyone happy, you have to think that, if you have a problem, not only do you lose revenue, but also you lose future revenue by not addressing the problem.

To grow their businesses, owners keep their eyes on the long-term bottom line. Joe always guarantees the quality of his work for every customer, even if this means going back and doing it again or giving away the work for free to keep the customer. He says he does this "because I know there are seven hundred more houses that this guy is going to build and I would rather lose one and gain six-ninety-nine." Hard work pays off over time when you work hard to satisfy customers, guarantee quality work, and don't give up on long-term goals.

Plan Purchases

Joe says one secret of his success is never turning business away. Recently, one of his managers told a customer that he was "too slammed." Joe told him, "We are never too busy. Even if you are too busy, you don't want your customer to know you're too busy."

Another strategy Joe employs to stay profitable is to look ahead when buying supplies. For instance, at the end of every year he's been in business, Joe takes his cash flow and buys enough material for the first quarter of the following year. By taking advantage of volume discounts, he gets a good price and has materials available for the first quarter of the year when construction work is slowest. He explains, "In the construction industry, the first quarter is the coldest quarter. You may not work as much, but if you're working, then you've got supplies."

Control Your Own Destiny

Joe says the idea of selling his business for a healthy profit has entered his mind recently, but he doesn't anticipate such a drastic change in his life any time soon. He adds that he's not ready to retire.

Joe explains that he wouldn't be where he is today if he had not taken the calculated risk of quitting his job at the grocery store, a choice that was only possible because he had started a side job that could become a viable full-time business. He explains that he was simply rising to the challenge of an opportunity: "The leverage I had was that I controlled my destiny. My motivation was not necessarily the financial part of it, but the challenge of creating that financial goal."

Top Takeaways

1. Work hard to make it work. Nothing will come to you easily. Satisfaction comes from the dedicated culmination of a quality job well done. You snooze, you lose.

2. Set high expectations. Don't settle for an unsatisfying life or job.

3. Look for opportunities to learn. Take advantage of the ideas and circumstances that cross your path.

4. Watch your bottom line. Being a business owner means taking care of your capital.

5. Stop putting money into somebody else's pocket. If you are gifted at what you do, find a way to put the money earned from your talents into your own pocket. Start small and grow. The marketplace will tell you if you have a successful idea.

6. Question people inside the industry. Knowledge is like gold. Do reconnaissance. Ask people for advice about everything.

7. Take calculated risks. Don't settle for a workplace that treats you unfairly or does not fulfill its promises. Set up an alternative, then get out while you can.

8. Create more ways to make money. Imagine new ways to do things. Innovate, then take action.

9. Focus on priorities. Take care of your family first and they will stay with you through the good and bad times.

10. Grow naturally with loyal customers. Saving money with practical purchases puts money into your pocket and helps you grow.

11. Plan purchases. Look at your natural cycles of buying and spending. Then work to find the best deals.

12. Control your own destiny. Challenge yourself with distant, reachable goals.

Chapter 12

How to Call It Quits Gracefully

nurture n. *the process of aiding and developing; teaching, coaching, mentoring, growing*

Every self-employed person measures success differently. We judge success by how happy we are, how well our home life and professional life are balanced, and how financially stable we feel. All of my friends and family members discussed in *Breaking Free* have shown me in numerous ways that they are not only satisfied and successful, but that they are also happy about the choice they made to start their own businesses.

After many years as a self-employed business owner, many entrepreneurs reach a point when they are ready to retire. The ending cycle of a business ownership situation can be a strange and challenging time. One person who recently made this transition very well is Rachel Beaupre, my aunt, who has been a role model all my life, in both family and business matters. Her successful transitions from employee to business owner to former business owner and employee hold many lessons for anyone wondering how positive self-employment adventures reach satisfying conclusions.

RACHEL BEAUPRE, 65—HAIR SALON OWNER

Forty years ago, Rachel was working in a hair salon in the cozy college town of Brunswick, Maine. When her boss decided to sell the shop, Rachel jumped at the opportunity. She bought the business. Suddenly, she quit working for somebody else and started working for herself as the owner of Looking Glass, a popular hair salon in downtown Brunswick.

Ten years ago, after thirty years as her own boss, Rachel sold her business to one of her employees, a fellow hairdresser who saw the opportunity for success. Today, Rachel has sold both the business and the building in which it is located. To say she is retired would be overstating her situation because she still styles hair at her former business. Although she doesn't own the business anymore, she still works a few days a week at the Looking Glass because she loves her trade and spending time working with friends, customers, and co-workers, some of whom she has known most of her life.

Rachel says her adventure into self-employment started with an opportunity she found while working in a full-time job she already enjoyed. "I had a job that was the job that I continued having, only I worked for myself. I opened up a salon that allowed me to work for myself and employ a couple of people." Job security and retirement plans were hard for a woman to find back in the 1960s, so she made the choice to improve her future prospects for both. But success did not come easily. She says, "I guess a lot of it was a passion for the job and a willingness to work hard, and also an ability to do it one day at a time."

Serve People Well

Rachel says working hard for her own business brought her great satisfaction: "Some days were more challenging than others, but there wasn't a day that I really didn't enjoy and love. Even though it's probably my most demanding child, it gave me a lot back, like all work should."

After graduating from high school, Rachel went to beauty school to become a hairdresser. Once she earned her license, she started working for nearby salons. She quickly earned a reputation as a dedicated worker with excellent skills. She also had enough experience to understand the hairdressing business.

For the next five years, she worked for the owners of a few local hair salons. When her second child, Jeffrey, was born, she started working in a salon near her house in Brunswick. This job move changed her life. She says: "That woman who owned that little salon became ill and wanted to sell it. So I bought it and turned it into a much larger salon through the years." During Rachel's thirty years as a business owner, the Looking Glass grew from a two-operator salon to a company with a staff of about fifteen.

Rachel says she has always thought of her business in terms of family. She explains:

> It was just a progression of things. It was kind of like a family that starts off at one place and you just keep adding on, so you add more bedrooms. The next thing you know, you're supporting a reasonably good-sized business for a little town. It's hard. It's like having fifteen kids: they all tweak a little differently and all their personal needs are all a little different, but basically, if you share the passion for the job, hopefully you serve them well.

Never Forget Supply and Demand

Although the small clientele from the business' previous owner helped Rachel get on her feet, she says her success as a business owner was built mostly on hard work and great staff:

> It came from just doing it and doing it and doing it. It builds on itself. It's like serving good ice cream, you know: somebody tells you it's good, so you try it out, and the next thing you know, you've got demand. Then you try to create the supply and demand. That's how something grows. You hope that you put out a good quality product, and that increases your demand. I guess that's pretty much the way it is in all business.

Rachel made the shift from employee to employer in less than one month. She had only been at the salon for three weeks when she bought it. The older woman who was selling it was at the end of her career. Rachel says:

She had started this little salon and couldn't run it anymore because of her illness. I looked at it as an opportunity. At the time I thought, better me than anyone. Why not me? With a little help, it wasn't a whole lot of money back then. It didn't require a lot of debt. It was set up.

Rachel's initial investment was something she could handle. For less than $10,000, she was able to buy a business that was already operational. After ten years at its first location, she bought a building in a better location. After she expanded the business to serve her growing clientele, she expanded the business again with more renovations to create more space. She says the growth was perfectly natural: "It was just one of those things that kind of fed on itself, with a clear plan that you needed to work with current dollars rather than borrowed dollars. That's what I always tried to do, is just build on the growth with money that was already in place for growth."

Set Long-Term Goals

One of Rachel's long-term goals was to own the building where she operated her business. She hoped to buy the existing building because of its great downtown location, but it was a rental that never became available for sale. Over the years she looked for a new location, but a suitable replacement was hard to find.

Sometimes finding the right business opportunity can take several years. It took Rachel a decade to find the perfect place to relocate her business. She wanted a place that was downtown, but it also needed to offer room enough to grow. She explains:

Most of the downtown buildings are pretty large. It was kind of cost-prohibitive for a small business to buy a large building, particularly in the relatively near area. So, when this little building became available, it was perfect because it had revenue upstairs, which was a dental office. It was large enough downstairs to create a salon that had doubled its size. And then we doubled again. It just kind of grew on itself.

Although Rachel admits that her own hard work played a vital role in building her business for three decades. She also relied on ethical business principles, such as being fair-minded and putting out a good product. She says, "All of these things kind of feed on themselves."

Never Look in the Opposite Direction

Rachel says she uses the same philosophy for dealing with occasional setbacks in her business plan, such as losing a good employee:

> There are three things that worked: I loved what I did, I had passion for it; I had good health; and I just never looked in the opposite direction. I think sometimes people look at other things as being greater and grander, and I always thought that I already had it. It's like living in Maine; you already live where you want to live, so why would you look elsewhere? Why would you fantasize about living in Hawaii when Maine gives you all you want? This is the way I felt about this business.

Rachel tried to run her business in a way that gave her the growth she wanted, the revenue she wanted, and a satisfying profession. She managed her company well enough to get all three. She says, "It's the old cliché: It isn't what you earn, it's how you spend. I tried to spend my dollars wisely and make them matter."

Appreciate "the Soul of the Business"

While working with many employees over the years, Rachel explains that her talented hairdressers are a big part of her success. "I tried to be fair-minded with staff, and was able to keep a lot of my staff a long time, which was certainly the soul of the business." Many hairdressers worked with her for more than twenty years, which is one of the many reasons Rachel feels her business is a success. She explains, "Eventually, everybody moves on. And so did I, but it was good." Today, under the leadership of one of her former employees, her business has reached the milestone of being in business for four decades.

It is difficult for any business owner to know when to retire from his or her business. Rachel knew she was ready to sell her business when she was ready to spend more time away from work. As an active mother, grandmother, wife, daughter, sister, and so on, Rachel had reached a point in her life where she wanted to spend more time with family and traveling. Because she knows businesses cannot be run from afar and they don't run themselves, she started to look at other options.

One day, ten years ago, one of Rachel's hairdressers said she was interested in buying the Looking Glass. Rachel saw an opportunity to live her new dreams of more travel and family time. She says:

> The time seemed to be right and the opportunity was there. She had cash in hand and paid me a very, very fair dollar for my business; more than I would have expected. Then, I still owned the building, so it gave me some revenue there. Just this past year I sold the building to the gal who owns the business. It was good. It's my retirement years, so this was good.

Build Friendships and Camaraderie

As one example of how much she loves her former business, Rachel continues to work at her old hairdresser's chair three days a week during the six months of the year when she's in Maine. Lately, she has been spending her winters in Florida with her husband, Dick. When she returns to Maine in the spring, she returns to the Looking Glass as an employee. "I enjoy the friendships and the camaraderie, and the little bit of cash flow is always nice. It still works for me. When it doesn't, then I'll know it's time to not go back."

Lately, whenever she returns to the salon to work, Rachel says, she's always reminded why she loves it. "Every time I go back, I think, yeah, this is good. I'm enjoying this." She also enjoys going home at night without the additional responsibility of managing the business. She says, "There's really nothing, once I leave there, that I have to really think about."

Love the Work

When Rachel started on her career path more than forty years ago, she had no idea where it would take her. When she was a young girl, she found her niche. She saw hairdressing as a perfect way to earn a living, meet people, and grow her skills. In 1961, the year she graduated from Brunswick High School, Rachel started taking classes in beauty school. "I tried it, liked it, and never looked back. There hasn't been a time that I haven't really enjoyed the work."

Some days were harder than others, she says, "but I've always loved the work: no regrets."

Work with Suppliers and Other Stakeholders

When she was growing her business, Rachel's marketing for the Looking Glass was primarily word of mouth. Over the years, she also tried many other forms of advertising. She tried many forms of media, but repeat business and referrals were her biggest sources of customers. She explains that quality work sells itself:

> You hopefully satisfy clients that come in and it builds on itself. You can advertise all you want, but if you don't deliver the product, then you're not going to get repeat business, and that's what you look for. I think you've got to get your name out there, but at the same time, you've got to put out what you promise. Hopefully we did that.

Relying on more traditional marketing methods, Rachel never started a Web site for her business, and it continued to grow without one.

Rachel's suppliers also helped her with many aspects of her marketing. She says, "A lot of the people that you work with, a lot of your suppliers, help you a lot with that, with just marketing and helping you retail, and all of that, and keeping your bottom line strong and healthy."

Save First and Pay Yourself Last

Because of the high price of labor, new business owners need to be versatile, and willing to do every job that comes up. Rachel grew her business doing many of the odd jobs that cropped up, and working hard every day. She says:

> That's true with any job, but working for yourself, make sure you spend your dollars wisely. If you need help with that, there are lots and lots of agencies, nonprofit and so on, that will help you with that. Use your resources the best you can, whether that's within house or whatever, and keep

looking toward the growth of the business. And pay yourself last. Save first and pay yourself last.

One way Rachel saved money and prepared for the future was by buying her building and paying her mortgage every month until it was paid off.

Another source of Rachel's success was the way she managed her organization. Knowing good leadership starts at the top, she always tried to be a good leader for her people by helping them grow and enhancing how they worked and lived. Her relationships with those employees, customers, and friends continue to thrive today. She says good leaders attract good employees: "If you have a reputation, you hopefully will just attract that kind of staffing, and your reputations are that you're fair-minded, you pay your bills, people want to do business with you. It's just built on good stuff; stuff you grew up with."

Stay Current

Staying on top of the advancements and changes in her field is another way Rachel continues to enjoy her successful career. She says continuing to learn new information is crucial to people in her industry:

> It's a very current business. You've got to stay current. What I love is, I've always worked with young people, and young people draw you into current, because that's who they are. You see the [styles] that come off the street, and that's what they want, and therefore you just kind of adapt.

Classes are a crucial way business owners stay up to date on changes in their industry. Even today, Rachel is on her way to a class on the latest hair-coloring techniques offered by one of the Looking Glass' suppliers. She says taking the class is a practical decision. "The price is right, so there was no reason not to go. They've got some new adaptations on color, so I thought, well, I can give that a couple of hours." Although nobody requires her to take these classes, they help her stay up to date with the latest styles, which helps her make a difference with her customers.

Hire Professionals

We all have our areas of strength and weakness. Recognizing them and filling in the gaps with employees and other assistance is crucial to success. To help her stay ahead of her finances and paperwork, Rachel hired an accounting firm. She explains: "There's nothing worse than finding out that you've neglected some kind of government form, or government payment, which is even worse. You can only do so many things, and the rest you have to hire professional people for." Good-quality support systems, including financial help, keep business owners afloat and out of trouble. A good business plan includes resources for these vital people and their services.

One of Rachel's main goals through her life and business has been to be a good person. She explains, "I always like to think that I've been kind along the way. I'd like to think that I didn't ever drop the ball on that, but if I had, then I would be sorry for that."

Part of reaching that goal is learning not to stress out about other people's perspectives. When Rachel encounters people with different ways of thinking, she says she tries to appreciate what makes each person unique: "You can celebrate that, as opposed to thinking of it as something that isn't as healthy. It's very healthy."

Although running her business and watching it grow was satisfying, Rachel says she also enjoyed stepping aside:

> I feel blessed actually, on lots and lots and lots of levels. Work has been great. I'm glad that it's at the end of my work life, because I'm ready to play more. But, that being said, there were times when I would have worked before I would have played, and now I'm ready to play before I work!

When Rachel was working full time in her salon, she often worked more than sixty hours per week. Looking back, she says working so many hours was just what it took to run a successful business:

> If cleaning staff didn't show up, you were it. If somebody couldn't work that day and it was your day off, you were it. That was just part of running a business. You have to be on every day. That's why other things, unfortunately, get put

aside. You've got to be willing to sacrifice that time in order to get the prize at the end. That didn't bother me at all. I just wanted to make sure that I didn't overlook things that I should have noticed.

Balancing work and family life is hard for all self-employed people, especially those with busy storefronts and large staffs. Rachel always tried to make sure her children never suffered because of her long hours at work. Looking back, she says, "I probably would have lightened up a little bit on that, but I did what I did because I thought that, when you're pretty much the sole owner and sole proprietor of a business, you do jobs. And that's what you've got to do."

Have Faith and Do the Best You Can

One clue that Rachel's strategy worked is her close relationship with her husband, Dick; her children, Alane and Jeffrey; and their families. During the six months she lives in Maine each year, her children live close enough to her to play a large role in her daily life. When she and Dick are in Florida during Maine's coldest months, their family visits them there.

Enjoying the benefits of her self-employment adventure, including many healthy relationships and two happy homes, Rachel remains humble about her success. She says, "Sometimes it's just kind of a little dumb luck, a little trust, a little handing it over to a higher power at some point. And have trust in the fact that you're doing the best you can, so let go of what you can't do more about."

Make Retirement Plans

Rachel explains that she was able to retire in part because of her investment in the building where her business is located. Although she did not create a formal retirement savings plan while she was in business, her investments in her business and other properties have allowed her to maintain a comfortable nest egg for the next part of her life. Every self-employed person has to consider an alternative to an employer's pension plan. Rachel says, "You have to plan that for yourself."

Retirement security for Rachel came in the form of smart investments. The cash from selling her business helped her and Dick retire, but the additional money from the sale of her building makes their retirement together much more comfortable. She explains: "It was a very good investment. It's worked out very well, and it's allowed us to move on and do other things."

Satisfy Customers

Part of the satisfaction Rachel received from her business came from knowing that she satisfied many customers over the past forty years. She takes pride in the fact that people still speak well of her business. Although maintaining her growing business was hard work, some days were harder than others. And some days, she says, were just pure entertainment:

> It's like kids. Some days you say, was it fun having kids? And you say, well, yeah, part of it was. Was it hard? Sure. Did it make you laugh? Sure. Did you shed some tears? Sure. It's all of the above. It's a real mixture of all kinds of things, like anything you have passion for. If you felt indifferent, then you wouldn't have any of those emotions, but when you feel passionately about something, all those emotions play in.

Now that she is on the other side of a business she started forty years ago, Rachel says all of those struggles were absolutely worthwhile. She created a job she loved and continues to love. Otherwise, she says, she would stop doing it. She explains:

> I feel badly for people who work at a job for thirty or forty years and just hate it. And I think, how sad is that? Because we are so lucky to have what we have, I've never fallen in that category. I've felt passion for the things that I did and continue to do, and continue to do it in that way. When I don't feel like that anymore, I'll just stop.

Make Great Decisions

Like many business owners, Rachel says, on a personal level, her decision to start her own business was one of the best decisions she ever made. She says she still loves her business:

Was it as satisfying? Yes. Was it hard? Yes. Would I love to have a pension from L.L Bean? Yeah!

I think everybody works hard for their dollars. What you have to do is plan accordingly.

Top Takeaways

1. Serve people well. Treat your employees like family and they will be more motivated and productive than if you treat them otherwise.

2. Never forget supply and demand. Keeping an eye on these two essentials of business can help you determine what you need to do to increase both and grow.

3. Set long-term goals. Once you get what you want, look to the future for other possibilities that will help you in the long run.

4. Never look in the opposite direction. Keeping your long-term goals in sight can help you avoid worrying about whether the grass is greener on a different path.

5. Appreciate "the soul of the business." Treat people fairly and they will stick around.

6. Build friendships and camaraderie. You'll know your business is great when you can sell it to somebody else and still work there for fun and profit.

7. Love the work. When you find a passion that grabs you, stay with it. Then find a way to turn the work you love into a self-employment situation.

8. Work with suppliers and other stakeholders. Learn everything you can from the people with whom you work to stay on top of industry trends.

9. Save first, and pay yourself last. Saving money gives you cash to put aside or invest. Paying your bills on time is an essential way to save money by avoiding interest and fees.

10. Stay current. Listen to your customers and suppliers for the latest information that can help you compete in a changing marketplace.

11. Hire professionals. If you need help, hire a professional accountant, plumber, roofer, lawyer, or whatever, before you get in over your head.

12. Have faith and do the best you can. Trust, faith, and hard work can prevent anxiety and help you find satisfaction in your work.

13. Make retirement plans. If you don't want to work forever, make investments that can help you retire when you are ready to be done.

14. Satisfy customers. When you feel a passion for your job, your customers will recognize it and come back for more.

15. Make great decisions. Decide what satisfies you; then create a plan.

Epilogue

Famous Last Words

salud interj. *to your health; a toast*

Not so amazingly, all of the people whose adventures are chronicled in *Breaking Free* repeat similar themes with many wide variations. Every entrepreneur who succeeds works hard: Persistence and stamina are vital if you want to succeed. The intertwining of that effort with the nurturing of positive relationships in our lives is what turns hard work into a satisfying life, and each of these examples is proof.

We all look at our competition and learn from others, but the ways we put these attributes into action are completely personal, like an intricate calculus that determines how well we get along with and work with others. A realistic, written plan helps immensely, or at least a dream that includes a profit. Looking beyond the complicated dynamics that play out in every business and personal relationship, success in life, family, and business comes about when we connect with others and work together for some common causes from which we benefit together, personally, professionally, and socially. When we do it our own way and we succeed, the fruits of our labor are even sweeter. None of these people say starting their own business was a mistake. Every one of them says it was one of the best decisions he or she ever made. With that kind of certainty, we've made self-employment work, and we're happier for it.

Those of us who have started our own businesses are as different as we are alike, but we share an autonomy that those working for others will only figure out when they try it for themselves. Most business owners value that autonomy so much, once we've found it, we do everything in our power to keep our businesses profitable so we can maintain that joy of independence for as long as we can; maybe even forever. Working for ourselves gives us a great feeling like no other. Part of that satisfaction is mastering the flexibility in time our work allows. That flexibility is a vast challenge successful business owners have somehow—personally and socially—figured out how to manage. Everyone has his or her own management methods, and, for whatever reason, they work for him or her. Success comes from both emulating others' successes and charting our own path into unknown territory. But it's not for us to judge our own business success. Our customers and our families are the true judges of our success. They reflect our success in their own successes.

Like beauty, success is in the eye of the beholder. For a business, it's also in the wallets of customers and the satisfaction of employees. Each of the people featured here have shown me through long and rich relationships that they are truly successful in many ways, with happy family lives, vibrant businesses, and contagious positive attitudes that spread to others wherever they go. I've talked to their customers, and they love these people, too. We might all have our unique traits and idiosyncrasies, but we're all people I hope you would want to meet, or work with.

I hope the strategies, clues, tips, techniques, platitudes, and principles described in this book help you build a sense of independence that is a beauty to behold. And if you really are considering going into business for yourself, I also hope that the stories I've collected help you think through the big issues and build some confidence when you look into yourself and ask, "If this guy can do it, and all of these real people with normal lives can do it, why not me?" And once you plan your future and put your plan into action, please don't forget to enjoy your exciting adventure on your way to making your dreams a reality. Salud!

References

Creating You and Company by William Bridges.
The One-Minute Entrepreneur by Ken Blanchard.
The 8th Habit by Stephen Covey.
Small Giants by Bo Burlingham.
"A Theory of Human Motivation" by A. H. Maslow.
Think and Grow Rich by Napoleon Hill.
U.S. Census Bureau's 2008 Current Population Survey (CPS).
The Wealth of Nations by Adam Smith.

Index

About the Author

CHRIS LAUER, in 2006, for the second time in his life, quit his job for a large publishing firm and started his own company. Today, he is the editor in chief who owns and operates Lauer Editorial Services (www.laueredit.com). The first time he quit his job to work for himself, back in 1992, he resigned from his writing and editing position at the *SF Weekly* in San Francisco. He quit so he could move to Eureka, California, where he was self-employed for six years as a publisher, editor, and writer of the regional arts and entertainment monthlies *Edge City Magazine* and *Anthem Monthly*. He was also a news reporter for KIEM-TV, the NBC affiliate in Eureka, California. He is the author of *The Management Gurus*, published in July 2008 by Portfolio. Now he lives and works as a freelance writer, editor, and author in Wilmington, Delaware. His e-mail address is delawareeditor@aol.com.